D1564850

Ticket

KIMBERLY KYSER

TICKET

A Guidebook

for

the Table

MORTARBOARD PRODUCTIONS
CHAPEL HILL, NORTH CAROLINA

Manufactured in the United States of America
First edition, first printing

Library of Congress Control Number: 2015912668
ISBN: 978-09965715-0-0

For Georgia and Trevor

and

In memory of my sister Carroll

Contents

The predictability of manners (if *this* is happening,
we must all do *that*) makes us interlock with each other,
all act in concert. We connect, in addition, with events,
dates, shared emotions, kinship and group ties, the life
cycle, the world in general. Conventions, as the word
suggests, come together.

—Margaret Visser, *The Ritual of Dinner*

Preface

Chapel Hill, North Carolina, is a progressive university town called "the southern part of heaven." Thank heaven it is the town that I call home. Growing up in this academic community, I took for granted the genteel southern manners and mores that were integral to the culture. Mine was a world of traditions: courtesy was next to godliness, family was supreme, and the seated evening meal was a sacred ritual that anchored each day. As children, my two younger sisters and I took turns setting the table where no books or toys were allowed during dinner, and certainly no bobbing up and down for second helpings or to answer phone calls. We were taught to sit up straight, put our napkins on our laps, use our utensils properly, ask that salt and pepper be passed to us rather than lunge across the table, and in all things to say "please" and "thank you." We engaged in normal, playful conversation with adults and responded "Yes, sir" and "Yes, ma'am." Instead of bolting from the table at the end of dinner we asked, "May I be excused, please?" and patiently waited for a response. The etiquette of dining was the structural underpinning for the spontaneity of our lively communions. And lively they were!

My father, Kay Kyser, was a big band leader and entertainer in the 1930s and 1940s well-known for his NBC radio and TV shows, "The Kollege of Musical Knowledge," his "Ol' Professor" persona, and wacky films. By the time my sister Carroll and I were in kindergarten, he was completely retired from public life and had moved us out of the limelight into his welcoming home state and the village of Chapel Hill, population 9,000. My father's University of North Carolina education, devotion to family, and Baptist background defined his values. And as you might expect, he was from a long line of teachers, university professors, and professionals. With old-school notions of child rearing, he was at once a strict taskmaster and iconoclast, and one of the funniest people you would ever meet—confusing characteristics in a middle-aged man who dressed in coat and tie and insisted on formalities such as standing up when an adult came into the room and addressing parents of friends as "Mr. and Mrs." He politely corrected fans or acquaintances who were too familiar: "You may call me Mr. Kyser."

Behind closed doors "Mr. Kyser" was not always formal, and the dinner table became his stage. The occasional swinging of his fork in the air while talking at table was a deliberate act to provoke giggles from us, the peanut gallery, and to tease my mother. "Kay, stop it! You are setting a bad example for the girls!" Tucking the linen napkin into the neck of his shirt was rebellion, too: he knew better, but he could control his mischievousness only so long. With deadpan delivery and the comedic timing of a true showman, he sat quietly listening to the all-female dinner chatter, waiting for the right moment to interrupt with jokes, puns, and irreverent but never vulgar stories as well as serious ones that taught values dear to his heart. He wove seamlessly into our conversations corrections of grammar, comportment, and misguided thinking.

My mother was Georgia Carroll, the first high-fashion supermodel discovered by famous New York agency owner John Robert Powers. He named her "The Most Beautiful Woman in the World." Instantly successful, she graced the covers of *Vogue*, *Harper's Bazaar*, *Cosmopolitan*, *Redbook*, to name only a few, and was the face of the American Red Cross during the Second World War. After a brief acting career at Warner Brothers and MGM in Hollywood, she met my father when they worked together on the War Bond Tours and USO shows for the troops.

During one performance at a base camp in the California desert (a show that luckily was captured on film for us to see today), my father excitedly announced to thousands of eagerly awaiting soldiers, "And n-o-w, here is gorgeous Georgia Carroll!" Deafening applause, wild cheering, and wolf whistles erupted as she walked on stage dressed in a tight sweater and flirty short skirt to pick the winning raffle number from a fishbowl filled with ticket stubs. Years later my father loved to say with a suppressed smile and cheeky twinkle in his baby-blue eyes that when he took one look at her in that outfit, he thought, "Now there's a girl who can cook." She became lead singer for his orchestra, and although fourteen years his junior, she became his leading lady in life: they married in 1944. Despite my father's facetious remark, Mother *did* become an accomplished cook and true gourmet. I used to tease that her taste buds were worthy of the Smithsonian!

At our house we had what southerners called "help," including someone who cleaned up after dinner. But no hired help, friends, or relatives could ever cook to my mother's satisfaction. She insisted on doing her own shopping and cooked everything herself. And no wonder: she had studied at Le Cordon Bleu Institute in New York City. At home in Chapel Hill our everyday menus were inspired by French cuisine and, occasionally, southern specialties to please my father. My sisters and I were thrilled when Mother baked our stately layered birthday cakes and decorated them with not only our names but also elaborately detailed flowers trailing from baskets or a trellis overflowing with Confederate jasmine made entirely of icing. With much attention paid to the preparation of food, presentation and consumption required equal respect. Reverence for the table and a love for all things associated with dining were thus ingrained and taken seriously.

Mother had a wonderful sense of humor and, like my father, told stories with a purpose. Two of her memorable stories were about manners. In the first, a sophisticated

New York hostess presiding over a formal dinner party noticed that a guest cutting his meat had lost control of his knife, which skidded across the plate and scattered peas onto the table in front of him. Without missing a beat, the hostess took her knife and pretended to make the same mistake, sending peas onto the table around her plate. Graciousness is saving face for others.

The other story was about a mother who explained to her daughter that a very nice woman called Mrs. Jones would be coming to tea. "Now, darling, I want to warn you ahead of time that Mrs. Jones has a very large, unusual nose." She took the child's hands in hers and, looking into the child's eyes, then earnestly and painstakingly continued, "Please, please don't stare at her nose." The child nodded in agreement, "Yes, Mother."

Mrs. Jones arrived, exchanged greetings with the mother and daughter, and was ushered into the sitting room where they chatted until it was time for tea. The mother moved the party to the tea table, which was beautifully arranged with a plate of cucumber sandwiches and another plate filled with scones and small individual bowls of jam and heavy clotted cream. Holding the silver teapot in her right hand and the fine bone china teacup and saucer in her left, the mother poured the tea oh-so-correctly, ceremoniously. She then placed the teapot on the silver tray and, still holding the cup and saucer as one is required to do, she turned to Mrs. Jones and asked, "May I offer you cream or sugar in your nose?"

I can still see my beautiful mother with her perfect nose and toothpaste-ad-pretty smile curled up coyly on the chintz-covered sofa in our sunny family room reciting this story to a small audience—my sisters and me and a few girlfriends from the neighborhood. She ended it with her breathy-silent laugh but offered no moral to the story, at least not that I can remember. Was this tea fable to be read as a catty put-down, or was it to be given a more kindly interpretation, an admonition that when we concentrate too hard on *not* taking the wrong step, that is precisely when we fall down?

Like my father, I am a devoted North Carolinian and call myself a native. I now speak, think, write about the South with a capital *S*. While my ancestry is southern on both sides, I am a confusing hodgepodge of "southern" influences. I was born in southern California—Hollywood, to be exact. After my family moved back east and settled in Chapel Hill for the school year, we returned to Beverly Hills for the entire summer. This was partly to escape the heat of North Carolina before air-conditioning, to be with friends and family who had relocated to California. "It was a weaning away time," as Mother described it years later, a gradual good-bye to the glamorous life. When I turned thirteen California was no longer the focus and the family summered in Europe. The crossings—and there were many over the years—were on the last of the grand ocean liners including the S.S. *France*, whose first-class Chambord dining room was called the greatest restaurant in the world. As the name suggests (Chambord is the sixteenth-century French Renaissance chateau built by King François I), the sumptuous food and ceremonious service were fit for a king and his court. In the evenings we dressed formally to dine on *la grande cuisine* in the classical nineteenth-century tradition of Carême (1784–1833) and Escoffier (1847–1935), modernized very little for gourmets of the 1960s. The *maître d'hôtel principal* ruled the Chambord dining room. His highly trained assistant *maîtres* and captains in formal attire politely explained the complex menu to guests and guided our orders while keeping an eye on the servers lower in the hierarchy: the *commis* who delivered food from the kitchen and the *garçons* who served with elegance and style. My "Irish twin" younger sister, Carroll, ordered with abandon: lobster, quenelles, vichyssoise, paté, *mille-feuilles* (Napoleons), Gateau Saint-Honoré (cream puff cake), you name it. Nothing was too exotic for Carroll. The *France* provided otherworldly dining experiences that I shall never forget, though I regret that much of the *cuisine classique* was lost on me. With adolescent rigidity I ordered grapefruit, steak, and ice cream almost every night—hardly *haute*!

Mother planned our life-altering travel. While in her early 30s with three small children at home, she enrolled in the University of North Carolina to pursue a bachelor's degree. "Education" reinforcing her college course work conveniently justified our long summers in Europe. Everything she studied rubbed off on us one way or another. And it was not just the immersion in history, art, and architecture: simply living the European experience was formative. These were my teenage years, after all—a time for observing and learning through osmosis what to do when, particularly at the table, where Europeans take proper manners seriously and are quick to judge when manners are lacking. It was in this period, and when I studied in the south of France during college, that I adopted the Continental style of holding cutlery.

At a simple restaurant in the French countryside, I watched a boy my age peel an orange with surgical precision using his fork and knife, never touching the fruit with his hands. After sleeping a night in rented rooms in an Austrian working class high-rise our family of five crowded onto wooden benches at a small kitchen table for breakfast. Our hosts spoke no English, and we spoke not one word of German. Dressed in trousers held up by suspenders and a sleeveless undershirt, the man of the house ate in silence while my sisters and I practiced our best table manners over bowls of oatmeal and slabs of hard bread, and my father entertained the group with pantomimes. Dining at the Danieli in Venice, if I asked for ketchup, or if my father demanded ice or, much worse, iced tea, or my sisters and I laughed too loudly—mostly at my father's vivid imitations amid recitations of the day's funny events—Mother scolded, "Don't be the Ugly American!" This was shorthand for "Blend in! Don't be loud." We were guests in a foreign country; being loud and demanding American creature comforts, especially while dining, is rude.

Comportment and consideration that put others at ease were my mother's concern. My father certainly was in agreement with her, yet his sights were set on the big picture: he saw to it that his all-female brood felt confident and at ease at any table, high or low. He of all people knew the value of adaptability. Well-traveled in the United States and abroad, my parents knew from experience that international travel—especially diverse dining experiences that bring one face-to-face with cultural differences—teaches respect for customs and heightens sensitivity to context. They insisted on our learning etiquette, including table manners, not so much for appearance's sake but because knowing *what* to do *when* is liberating: we can relate to people, all kinds of people, directly without being distracted by mechanics.

While writing this preface and recalling how I learned table manners, I asked myself what relevance my story, and indeed table manners, have today? I'll answer with the aid of a quote I found in a magazine in the waiting room of my dentist's office, words by the wine critic and cookbook author Matt Kramer that inspired an "aha moment." Kramer laments the loss of social ritual and gets directly to the heart of the matter: "In our collective preference for casual we lose a bit of ceremony, of ritual and, not least, a kind of pause for a daily form of beauty." Daily beauty is the heart of the matter. The table and the manners we bring to it transform the fulfillment of a biological need into a social if not an aesthetic experience that, with just a little forethought and effort, feeds body and soul.

Young readers, you are living in a fast-paced, multicultural world that differs in many ways from the world of my generation; yet you will be surprised how little the fundamentals of courtesy have changed. They are universal, especially when it comes to the ritual of dinner.

Table manners and thoughtful behaviors associated with dining are timeless and exceedingly important for a variety of interpersonal and professional reasons. You may be pleasantly surprised to discover the ease with which you can learn the rules of the table and cultivate the self-confidence that comes with being a skilled dinner partner. Happy reading and *bon appétit, buon appetito!*

Acknowledgments

When I first began writing this book I envisioned a compact book of instructions. Yet the more research I did, the more interested I became in the history of table manners and the evolution of courtesy. My studies in the Italian department at UNC, which began in 2002, were an impetus in this regard, and I thank Dr. Ennio Rao for fostering my interest in Italian language and culture.

My thanks go to those who contributed their time, talent, ideas and support along the way—first of all, my niece Amanda Bryan and my friend Ben Thompson, both early supporters of this project and also hand models for my photographic illustrations. For reading and editing the early stages of the book and for his advice, I give special thanks to Dr. Neal McTighe. I am so very grateful for Laura Cotterman's expert copyediting and for her patience and Julie Allred's guidance and book design. My readers of the completed manuscript Amanda Kyser, Raymond Farrow, Chuck Lovelace, and Dr. Ennio Rao offered much appreciated feedback and encouragement. In addition, I would like to thank Chuck Adams, my daughter Georgia Carr, Artie Dixon, Dr. Brandon Essary, Greg Fitch, Lori Harris, Kathy Hendricks, Pete Hendricks, Robin Hutchison, Matt Liberti, Elizabeth Harriss MacDonald, Holland MacDonald, Beth Mauldin, Paula Meyer, Maxine Mills, Pam Morrison, Moreton Neal, Tim Noonan, Shannon Ravenel, John Sherer, Dr. John Sweet, Elizabeth Woodman, and Douglas Zinn.

My son Trevor Carr keeps me "real" with regular merciless critiques of *my* manners, chastising me if I fidget with the salt and pepper or take too big a bite of salad when we eat together at my kitchen table. Trevor, thank you for making me laugh!

Special thanks go to Chuck Lovelace, executive director of the Morehead-Cain Foundation at UNC–Chapel Hill, who invited me to explain table manners to a group of young scholars. *Ticket* grew out of this talk. An article I wrote for publication a decade ago inspired my idea for a small reference book on table manners, which then simmered on the back burner for many years until this moment of talking to the students. Hearing their enthusiastic reactions reignited the fire.

I owe so much to St. Catherine's School in Richmond, Virginia, where I spent my last two years of high school. There, in the strictest environment, a rigorous academic education was paired with training in social skills and community service. We wore one style of uniform by day and changed into another for the evening meal. In the dining hall, alternating groups of students worked as the waitstaff in two-week shifts, which taught us how to serve properly and how to be served. It was at St. Catherine's that I began to value the training and exposure my parents had provided.

With that said, I would like to thank my parents, Georgia and Kay Kyser. I thank my mother for the finger-bowl drills and other refinements; her insatiable appetite for learning and curiosity about the world; her passion for cooking, the arts, and all that is beautiful. I am so grateful for my father and his grounding: for his encouraging me to think, to laugh, to write (it was he who taught me how to write a proper thank-you note!), and for his insistence that my sisters and I feel confident and at ease at any table.

Introduction

"You have beautiful table manners," said the *soigné* European artist to his luncheon partner, my niece Amanda. "Thank you," she said with her usual poise, unusual for an American college student. "I can't wait to tell my aunt."

"She certainly raised you right," he replied.

That luncheon was ten years ago and of course I have never forgotten the compliment. In the privacy and safety of home, my sisters and I had practiced the choreography of dining until it became second nature. I wished the same for my own children, nieces, and nephew. Talking about manners is a tricky business, and teenagers never want to be corrected or told to do almost anything, so I certainly got my share of dirty looks, sighs, and pushback on the table manners issue. "Who cares?!" my son snapped. "You're out of touch!" Like, "fuhgeddaboutit!"

I tried to think of a lighthearted way to teach and preach. "Table manners are like dance steps," I said with a smile (and those who know me well realize that sometimes I'd rather dance than eat). "Once you've learned them, you never again stare at your feet, but instead, gaze into the eyes of your dance partner. You know which foot goes where, which turns to make moving in time with the music and in concert with others on the dance floor. That is what a good dinner party feels like if guests know their manners. With a little practice you won't have to think about *what* to do *when*. If you misstep—pick up the wrong fork or take too big a bite—it's not a catastrophe!"

If I had known then what I know now, I would have stated my case more forcefully, or at least alluded to something in their own experience. Judging from their reaction, the dancing metaphor was too old-fashioned for adolescents: the concept went in one ear and out the other. Kids love monsters and horror movies, so perhaps a passage about rituals during cannibal meals from Margaret Visser's *The Ritual of Dinner* would have gotten their attention: "Every human society without exception obeys eating rules." Yes, even cannibals. Describing Aztec cannibal meals as extremely formal (never mind the gruesome details), she adds, "Indications are that more ritual usually governed the eating of people than was found necessary at ordinary meals." Of course, when the entree is George *grillé au beurre blanc* or Boiled Betty, it is difficult—unthinkable—to call these rules table manners or that particular society human. Visser continues: "But every dinner eaten with others requires rules, and these soon become elaborated into a system of table manners, which are ritual where eating is concerned." Eating rules are here to stay, but many young adults (all ages, really) ignore them and ask why they are so important. I hope that this book will answer that question.

Table manners are an acquired skill that many of us are taught by parents or in school. We learn them by heart through practice and self-awareness. No one arrives in this world with an etiquette chip embedded in the brain. Without either instruction or an innate talent for observation and imitation, the untutored person functions in ignorant bliss, unaware that her dinner partners may not share her great happiness. With chest-beating bravura, others simply defy eating rules and either do not notice or don't give a flip that, with hair standing on end, their companions are aghast at their caveman-style eating. We all make mistakes, little blips that, thankfully, are forgiven; but defiance is a bomb, not a blip, and hard to overlook. Affected teacup-and-curtsey suavities are one thing, and I can understand the urge to reject them. On the other hand, streamlined table manners promote good communication, put dinner companions at ease, and demonstrate self-control and social awareness. "People making money know that good impressions can facilitate the making of more of it, whereas an image wanting in the proprieties can actually get in the way," writes Visser. "Where aspiration has definite chances of leading to success, decorum and inhibition lose their connotations of repression and pretentiousness, and take on suggestions of honing, competence, confidence and speed." Especially in the context of earning a living and advancing one's career, these qualities are an asset.

Living in North Carolina's Research Triangle surrounded by thousands of college students, I learned quickly that streamlined table manners are not in the curriculum; in fact, few students pay attention to table manners at all. Hostile body language, fist-holds of cutlery, stabbing with the fork, and crude sawing with the knife—these make up a savage style that has become the new norm. The university community is aware of the deficit, and on several occasions I have been asked to speak to students about table manners and appropriate dress. (New hires and interns were showing up for board meetings in cutoff jeans and flip-flops!) These presentations inspired me to write this book.

A few years ago while I was hard at work on this book project, I attended a trustee dinner at the University of North Carolina. During the soup course, I turned to my charming dinner partner on my left and introduced myself. We chatted about his work in the corporate world, his new employment at the Kenan-Flagler Business School, and his family. Then he asked me what I was working on (drum roll...gulp). I don't know what came over me because I just came out with it: I told him that I was writing a table manners book for students but really for all ages. He looked stricken and asked in the most vulnerable tone, "You're not going to judge me, are you?" I laughed and said, "Of course not!" He then confessed that when he was in business school a course in table manners was required and the subject still made him nervous.

When the meat course arrived he noticed my injured hand and leaned toward me and whispered, "Would it be incorrect if I offered to cut your meat?"

"Oh, thank you. That is so nice of you, but I don't need help," I replied, surprised by the intrusion but grateful for his kindness. I joked with him about it and assured him that it was no problem. After a few minutes the real answer to his question came to me. I leaned toward him speaking quietly, directly in his ear: "*Never* is a thoughtful gesture incorrect."

Ticket is a guidebook to the table for university students and young professionals. It maps out a skill set that travels from dining room to boardroom and beyond. How you dress, speak, and present yourself contributes to your success and that of the occasion. The first chapter is called "Getting Ready" and suggests what to wear, what to take as your hostess gift, and what to say and do at the front door when introducing friends or coworkers to the host. "Tools of the Table" includes a brief history of cutlery followed by instruction in how to hold the fork, knife, and spoon and a discussion of the American versus Continental styles. "The Formal Dinner" explains step by step how to navigate dinner served in multiple courses. Although the seven-course dinner is the most formal and includes a palate-cleansing sorbet course after the fish course, I guide the reader through a six-course meal, omitting this step (it seems obvious how to eat a tiny dish of sorbet that arrives with its own small spoon). From the soup course to the finger bowl, there is a chapter for each, written in very simple language that even a student visiting from abroad can understand. At the suggestion of young friends who think it helpful to have some quick references, toward the back of the book is a catchall chapter called "A Review." The final chapter, "A Brief History of Courtesy and Table Manners," is a gallop through centuries of courtesy. My hope is that this final section will shed light on *how* table manners evolved in response to social, political, and technological change and explain *why* we do things as we do. Though customs change, table manners have persisted and will always be a mainstay of civilized conduct. Sources consulted for this book are listed in the References.

For the sake of efficiency I had to make a choice when referring to gender, and I apologize to the sisterhood that instead of "host and/or hostess," I use "host" intending gender neutrality. To clarify other terms, I use the more universal term "cutlery" instead of "flatware" or "silver-ware." I refer to "prongs" on the fork instead of "tines," which is also correct.

Acquiring good table manners is like learning correct English grammar or a foreign language, learning how to dance or to play music: study the formal rules first in order to creatively break them. Practice table manners at home. Think about what you are doing and how to make the dining experience pleasurable for others. I cannot overemphasize the concept of *observation*: self-awareness, social awareness. Before you know it you will be gliding effortlessly through seated dinners and having a wonderful time with dinner companions! Let's begin.

Getting Ready

Rsvp

Before we walk through the hours preceding the dinner party, double-check that you have replied to the invitation. A written invitation always requires a response and usually includes "Rsvp," written with only one capital letter because it stands for a sentence in French: *Répondez, s'il vous plaît*, please respond. So do just that. Make sure that you have replied to the invitation well in advance. Use the mail to respond to an invitation that was mailed, unless an e-mail address is offered below the host's Rsvp information. If the dinner party is small with a carefully orchestrated guest list, do not break the engagement at the last minute unless you are ill or a family member has died.

Dressing for Dinner

Everyone must dress according to his status and age, because if he does otherwise it seems that he disdains other people.... [A] man must also try to adapt himself as much as he can to the sartorial style of other citizens and let custom guide him even though it may seem to him to be less comfortable and attractive than previous fashions.
—Giovanni Della Casa, *Il Galateo*

First impressions are said to make or break you. That may sound harsh, but remember that how you present yourself is a powerful form of communication in a sound-bite world. Especially at a first meeting, evaluations come quickly. If you show up at dinner wearing something that takes your host's breath away or is disrespectful of the occasion, you send a message that you are either arrogant or oblivious, and in return you may receive a message you don't like: silence. You won't be invited back.

The dress code for every situation is contextual and constantly changing. In the past it was considered *déclassé*, and striving, to overdress in costume-like and attention-getting clothes. In the context of today's uber-casual style, many people, and especially students, confuse behind-closed-doors clothes like sweats or PJ's with street clothes. Clothing as skimpy and revealing as underwear in public is like an anxiety nightmare (many women dream that they went to graduation or gave a speech wearing only their slip, and my men friends say they experience the same—without the slip).

That the ubiquitous term *casual* is ill-defined and abused leaves us scratching our heads searching for guidance. *Informal* takes for granted *formal*. It means "not done or made according to a recognized form; irregular, unofficial, unconventional," says the *Shorter O.E.D. Casual* means haphazard, without formality or rules (but which ones are omitted, certainly not all of them?), and it essentially describes anything and nothing, except leave off the suit or the choker pearls. Young guests arrive at my house in sweaty, smelly gym shorts in winter and think nothing of sitting at the dining-room table dressed like this. It may be fun for the wearer but it really puts others on the spot.

"Cleanliness and purity always accompany the idea of eating, so clothes must be clean—and not sullied during the meal. Wearing clothes is a social act," writes Visser, "and (except for protection and warmth, neither of which is usually very necessary at dinner) has nothing to do with 'nature' or common sense. Clothes are an overlaying of the physical, like table manners themselves. They bow to social agreements (for example, in following fashion); they adorn their wearers and enhance their appearance, just as laying a table or decorating a dish helps make the meal aesthetically pleasing." When I go to the trouble and expense of cooking a great meal—cleaning up my house, decorating the table for guests to enjoy—it is disappointing that my guests arrive in clothes they would wear to clean out their garage. To dress up even just a little is a small gesture that contributes to the festivity and success of the occasion.

For a private party or one that is not overtly business-related, pay attention to the wording of the invitation. And consider who will be at the dinner party and in whose house or in what country you will be dining. These variables set the tone for what to wear. When your invitation says that you are invited to a "dinner party," dress up: coat and tie for men, dress and heels or fancy pants outfit for women. "Come for dinner" means something else that does not necessarily require festive dress, but certainly a change of clothes for the evening is appropriate, something that is a shift in mood from your daily grind. An invitation to a "luncheon" is decoded "dress up," whereas the costume-call for "Let's go to lunch or "Let's have lunch" depends on context—upscale restaurant or hamburger dive—and purpose of meeting over food (work-related, just catching up, or celebratory). If you're going to a picnic in the country, it is not the time to wear your little black dress and jewels; a Sunday luncheon party implies dressing up a bit and in some cases coat and tie for gentlemen and comparable formality for ladies; Sunday brunch is what I'd call "groomed casual," or sometimes "dressy casual." (Again, "casual" is difficult to pinpoint.) In either case it is really inappropriate to wear baggy jeans, an oversized sweatshirt with writing on the front and back, and gym shoes. At any age, this outfit is unflattering, looks unclean, and worst of all, communicates a certain disdain for the occasion—the fashion equivalent of "flipping the bird."

A person does not need complicated or expensive clothes to present well. Tailoring and good grooming transform the simplest apparel. At a casual dinner party it is a good rule of thumb that gentlemen wear a shirt with a collar, at minimum a polo knit shirt. In many settings, well-fitting jeans with a blazer or sport coat, dress shirt, and leather shoes are perfectly respectable for both men and women, although for ladies there is more room for individual style. But choose carefully. Always be mindful of your age and the formality of the occasion.

One rule for business socializing: dress according to your profession. "Whatever you wear, it must suit you and be compatible with your calling," remarked Renaissance courtesy author Giovanni Della Casa in 1558. "Otherwise a priest might dress like a soldier and a soldier a jester" (Della Casa 1986). The rules for bankers and lawyers are different from those for college professors or those in the arts, although all men look good in well-fitting suits and good shoes. For a business lunch meeting, a university trustee dinner, or your firm's holiday party, you are expected to already know how to dress. You are safe to err on the more formal side because it shows respect for rank and seniority, and as I have said before, dressing well contributes to the success of the event. If you are invited to the boss's house for a small dinner party, it is perfectly all right to ask, "What is the dress for tonight?"

Business attire, a term seen often on a variety of invitations to both professional and purely social events, means a suit and tie for men and for ladies a nice skirt suit, pants suit, or possibly a not-so-fancy cocktail dress. *Semiformal* means a dark suit, white shirt, tie, and polished black shoes for men and cocktail attire for women. *Business casual* for men in banking and the professions is interpreted as slacks (not jeans), a suit jacket or sport coat, and a dress shirt without the tie. In other words, for casual Fridays the jacket and pants do not have to match, and you leave off the necktie. I offer comparable advice to women, who have more choices and freedom of interpreting the category. It goes without saying that leather shoes, not gym shoes, are worn with business clothes.

In the past, an engraved invitation for a dinner, wedding, or dance after six in the evening signaled the wearing of black tie for men and evening clothes for women. In unspoken etiquette lingo, one purpose of the engraved invitation, other than requesting the pleasure of your company, is to communicate the specific dress code. Today few receive engraved invitations or would ever get the message anyway, so you have to spell it out: *black tie.* The formal evening attire is called "black tie" or "dinner jacket," and in America we also say "tuxedo." You may see advertisements for white tuxedos with pale blue ruffled shirts and hot pink ties, as I did on TV recently, but avoid this goofy costume and others like it you may see on the "red carpet." Stay with the traditional black tie. Although the double-breasted dinner jacket is a correct, retro style and flattering to a slim build, the preferred style is a single-breasted black wool dinner jacket without vents, peaked lapel or shawl collar, covered buttons. This is worn with the traditional black wool trouser that is a bit tapered with satin stripe or "braid" down the outside of each leg. The evening shirt with turn-down collar is worn with cuff links and studs and a black bow tie, hand-tied. No clip-on ties, please. A low-cut black evening vest or a cummerbund that used to be absolutely *de rigeur* are today regarded by some as optional. To be safe, if you are traveling abroad, avoid colors and novelty patterns for the tie, vest, or cummerbund. Wear black shoes that are highly polished leather or patent leather with laces. Choose the tuxedo style that suits you, but do wear one when the occasion calls for it. Men who make up their own rules and wear a business suit appear disrespectful of the occasion, a sort of party pooper.

Meeting and Greeting

The first moments at a dinner party or luncheon are made more enjoyable if you employ a few simple habits of meeting and greeting. The following directives are subtle and may seem insignificant, but they are important social cues.

They pay respect to the host and guests and will in turn reflect well on you.

First Words

Look the person in the eye and say one of the following:

"How do you do, Mrs. Jones?" (most formal and a bit archaic)
"How are you, Mrs. Jones?"
"I am very happy to meet you, Mrs. Jones."

When asked, "How are you?" respond, "I am fine, thank you," or "I am very well, thank you." Do not respond: "Good," or "I am doing good."

Shaking Hands

Shaking hands man-to-man is automatic and expected. When a man is introduced to a woman she may or may not extend her hand but simply say, "It is a pleasure to meet you." But if he extends his hand, she is obligated to follow through in order not to be rude.

Shaking hands woman-to-woman is becoming almost as common as man-to-man, especially among the young. In Europe handshaking is automatic; sometimes kissing on the cheek is too, but not in business settings.

A word about kissing as a greeting: there are many variations and prohibitions with kissing as a greeting. Double and triple kissing, starting with the right cheek, is friendly in some countries and shunned in others. It is warm and friendly if you know the person well, or well enough, and if it is a common practice in his or her country, as it is beginning to be in the United States. Air-kissing is regarded by most as an empty gesture, although sometimes I prefer it in order to avoid getting or giving a lipstick imprint on the cheek. To be safe, stay with shaking hands.

Rules of Introduction

Start by saying the person's name *to whom* you are making the introduction.

Remember that a man is introduced *to* a woman:

"Georgia, I would like to introduce *to you* my friend John."

"Mrs. Miller, may I introduce *to you* Dr. Bashford."

A younger person is introduced *to* an older person:

"Chancellor Caldwell, I would like for you to meet my son, Trevor."

A lower ranking person is introduced *to* a ranking person:

"President Obama, I would like for you to meet Ambassador Ferrero."

Response: "It is a pleasure to meet you, Ambassador Ferrero."

"How do you do, Ambassador Ferrero." (most formal)

For introductions at casual social events with family or among equals, it is much nicer to say: "Taylor, I'd like you to meet Ben," and *not* "Taylor, this is Ben" while pointing your thumb in his direction, as if hitchhiking.

The formal and respectful way to address another person who is your elder or of higher rank is to say Mr. or Mrs. (or his or her title) followed by the person's surname. Only use a first name when invited to do so. A word about nicknames: When a person introduces himself as Robert, do not reply, "Nice to meet you, Bob." Elizabeth is not "Beth," Susan is not "Sue," Kimberly is not "Kim," and so forth. Many people use their full given names exclusively, and it is presumptuous and disrespectful to assume otherwise. Nicknames are by invitation only.

Gifts for the Host or Hostess

To arrive at a dinner party with a bouquet of loose flowers is, in my opinion, disruptive. Flowers can be a lovely hostess gift if delivered the day or morning before the party or the day after as a thank-you present. Normally, a hostess has already arranged a centerpiece for the table and flowers for the house, so surprising her with cut flowers means that she must leave her guests to find a vase, trim the stems, and arrange the flowers—one added task to an already high-performance evening.

If you choose to bring white wine, prosecco, or champagne to a formal occasion, do not chill it. As with flowers and the menu, both planned ahead of time, wine for the evening has already been selected. Bringing cold wine sends the message that the host must serve it out of courtesy to you. And for goodness sake, don't go into the host's kitchen and put your bottle into the refrigerator! There is already enough hustle and bustle without adding confusion. There is an unspoken understanding that "refrigerator friends" is a designation for only the most intimate of friends.

For informal occasions everything changes. Milling around in the host's kitchen is part of the fun at a potluck supper or a casual dinner with friends, and chilled wine is a perfect gift. You are contributing to the meal, and if it is not needed, it can simply be received as a gift to the host. A "hostess gift" (that is the term used) does not have to be wine or food. Gifts may be something of interest to hosts that show you are paying attention to their preferences. I like to receive books, music, and consumable gifts, especially specialty foods and wines that go into the larder for use at another time.

Gifts are not a substitute for a handwritten thank-you note for formal dinners, including a dinner party at someone's house. Nothing is a substitute for the handwritten note of appreciation. The note can be short but must be timely—and *not* an e-mail. If you just *can't* find pen, paper, and a stamp, call the host the next day to say that the party was wonderful and you are so grateful to have been included. If you are unable to reach them in person, leave a voicemail. But do thank! A family member put me up to the next suggestion which I add *very* reluctantly. If *all* else fails (Perhaps even the smallest expression of gratitude is better than nothing at all?), resort to a letter-style e-mail: "Dear So-and-so,..." Make it a stand-alone "letter" and not folded in with business issues. Be forewarned that unless you are writing to someone out of the country, in which case e-mail makes sense, to some hosts an e-mail communicates a presumptuous and unappreciative attitude. (Do not even think of sending a text message!) One exception to the hard-and-fast note-writing rule is the big cocktail party. Then the personal note is optional and not expected, but always appreciated. I can assure you that observing this courtesy, or ignoring it, does not go unnoticed.

Cell Phone and Camera Use

> I know no one thing more offensive to a company, than
> inattention and distraction. It is showing them the utmost
> contempt; and people never forgive contempt.... For my
> own part, I would rather be in company with a dead man,
> than with an absent one; for if the dead man gives me no
> pleasure, at least he shows me no contempt; whereas the
> absent man, silently indeed, but very plainly, tells me that
> he does not think me worthy of his attention.—The Earl
> of Chesterfield, *Lord Chesterfield's Letters to His Son*

"Inattention and distraction" are rude and insulting, and were as problematic for Lord Chesterfield in the eighteenth century as they are today. Misuse of cell phones and cameras in social settings is distracting and disruptive, an indiscretion committed by all ages. Check your e-mail and messages before you arrive at your host's front door, and turn off the cell phone, all electronics, before the event. It is very distracting to have a guest stare at his lap to check e-mail or research a topic in the middle of a conversation, or worse, in the middle of a dinner party. This inattention to host and guests communicates disdain for the occasion, even if it is unintentional. You are taking up space but "absent" from the party. If you are waiting for a life-and-death phone call or text message, discuss this with the host before the meal begins and turn the phone to vibrate. If the call comes in, excuse yourself as you would if you needed to use the restroom by saying, "excuse me." Leave the room to talk out of earshot of the other guests. Announcing, "I need to use the restroom," or "I need to take a call," is disruptive and too much information. Otherwise, put the cell phone along with your keys in your purse or coat pocket, and do not bring them out again until you are on your way home.

Put your camera away as well. Taking photographs and videos with your smartphone or camera during a lovely meal is rude. It sends many messages, most of them insulting: that you are not in the moment, not engaged with the people around you. Unless you are eating lunch at the top of the Eiffel Tower and clearly in unbridled tourist mode and, more important, you have the approval of your traveling companions, picture taking is intrusive in dining rooms and restaurants and certainly inconsiderate of the host. Many upscale restaurants now ban photography.

Informality makes room for exceptions, and some casual restaurants like the local pizzeria are not bothered by photography. Even so, it is polite to ask ahead of time and engage a waiter to take the picture. At home, familial gatherings beg to be recorded, yet it is offensive to make a video or photo of someone eating (really any time) without their permission. The older you get the more you will appreciate this precaution.

Some things seem too silly to mention: do not put your cell phone, car keys, purse, or other personal effects on the dinner table! I have seen men and women, young and old, do this, most startlingly at a black-tie dinner dance. Small handbags rest in your lap under the napkin, and larger ones may be stored before dinner or laid at a woman's feet under the dinner table, well out of the way so that the server does not trip over them.

Conversation at the Dinner Table

The rule for *very* formal dining in America and on the Continent is that once seated at dinner, the hostess turns to the man on her right and begins a conversation. According to etiquette writer Amy Vanderbilt, "somewhere midway during the meal...she gently terminates her conversation with the gentleman on her right—the gentleman of honor—and turns to the gentleman on her left. Others are supposed to watch for this 'turn' and do likewise." A few courtesy writers propose that the turn occurs after completing the first course, and the back and forth continues with each course. This rule, called "turning the table," ensures equal conversation with both your dinner partners. Vanderbilt says that it "makes for conversational artificiality."

Today, unless you are at a state dinner or a very formal affair, the format is informal. As conversation is spontaneous, guests just begin talking, sometimes with several people starting a discussion together. If the table is small enough, you may talk (not shout) to those across it as well as to those on your right and left and in no particular order. You may have the turning-of-the-table rule in the back of your mind to make sure that you visit with both of your neighbors at the table, and I suggest that you adhere to this as a hard-and-fast rule. If you have a dull dinner partner, at minimum feign interest, for it is the kind thing to do. It is gracious and kind to also reach out to those who are not included in a conversation. If you are the one left alone, do not worry about intruding on an ongoing conversation near you. To engage in conversation is a way of contributing to the occasion. Asking questions of others (politely, without sounding like an interviewer) rather than focusing on yourself is a way to show interest in them and to practice the art of good listening.

An important bit of advice: turn down the volume. Learn to speak in modulated tones if you are dining in a formal setting or in a public place, and especially in a foreign country. The "Ugly American" that my mother loved to reference—and really the boorish person from any country—is loud and shrill at the table. Yelling across the table and, even worse, across the room to remind a friend not to forget his or her coat or to get a waiter's attention, makes a scene that disrupts others around you.

Speaking of making scenes, a lunch or dinner party is neither a therapy session nor reality TV. When you have just been introduced to someone, avoid prying questions about his or her marital status, age, or what happened to cause a physical defect. "Gaze not at the marks or blemishes of others and ask not how they came," is a maxim in *George Washington's Rules of Civility and Decent Behavior*. Don't offer descriptions of your own medical condition, your most recent operation, or details of a misfortune. Doctors and medical students, remember that you are not in a clinic but at the dinner table where graphic descriptions of procedures are nauseating. As my mother always said: "Please, no organ recitals!" Keeping dinner conversation on the up-and-up to accentuate the positive is a cardinal rule of good table manners that has been around for centuries. Consider this quote from *Il Galateo:*

> At parties and at mealtimes you should not tell sad
> stories or say anything to remind people of pain,
> illness, death, disease or other distressing subjects.
> If anyone lapses into a topic of this sort, you should
> gently and tactfully change the subject and suggest
> something more cheerful and suitable. Even so, as I
> once heard said by one of our neighbors, a man to be
> depended on, men should have as much need of tears
> as they have of laughter. He used to say that this was
> why the grim plays, which were called tragedies, were
> first compiled, and the purpose of them when they
> were recited in the theaters, as was done in those days,
> was to move to tears those who felt the need for them.

In this way, by weeping, they were cured of their disorders. But, however this may be, it is not right for us to grieve the hearts of the people to whom we are talking, especially on occasions which are meant for happiness and recreation and not for tears. And if you should know of anyone suffering from anxiety to weep, it is very easy to dose him with strong mustard or place him in a smoky room.... It is better to remain silent than to talk of matters which cause sorrow. (Della Casa 1986)

In some cultures, especially in Europe, the question "What do you do (for a living)?" is rude. It is too direct, too literal, and makes you look impatient, as if you are sizing them up. Many find this interrogation uncomfortable, especially these days. With our economic problems in the United States, you may surely put some people on the spot with, "What do you do?" The person you are talking to may have been laid off or not have found a satisfactory solution to employment and would rather not mix business discussions with pleasure. In the end, the indirect approach will yield as much if not more valuable information than rapid-fire questioning.

At a recent black-tie dinner (I sound as if I go to a lot of parties, but I don't!), a courtly southern gentleman introduced himself and his wife, quickly identifying himself as an attorney. We were standing, chatting, waiting for dinner to be served, and within minutes, perhaps three sentences into the conversation after asking me the ages of my adult children (no doubt to estimate my age, clever devil), he said, "Tell me about your career." Before I could catch my breath and organize an answer, someone walked up and interrupted the conversation and saved me from a sarcastic but metaphorically truthful reply: "I am a shepherdess and part-time volunteer firefighter."

A good conversationalist will instead attempt general, playful questions. "Tell me about yourself." "How do you spend your time?" "What do you do for fun?" "What is your passion in life?" Indirection is gracious.

Some things remain personal and are inappropriate for discussion at *all* social occasions. Do not broadcast to the table that you are on a diet. Former chief of staff to First Lady Jacqueline Kennedy, etiquette writer Letitia Baldridge, warns that your weight-loss diet must remain a secret, and so should your food obsessions. "For a guest to remark about the cholesterol content of the hostess's food or the caloric intake of sugar in coffee or a fattening dessert that you should resist makes everyone mad. You can make your host resolve never to let you join his luncheon group again if you rant and rave about fiber content, cancer-fighting vegetables, the fact that you have just lost another ten pounds, and why doesn't everyone else do the same, and so on. Mealtime is relaxation time."

The version of formal manners that I was taught embraces the notion of enjoying the food but not talking about it. If I have worked hard to make a wonderful meal, I very much appreciate a positive response, but I find it extremely tiresome to be around people who regard food as medicine and monopolize a group with a diatribe.

Enjoy the food and compliment the cook but do not ask for the recipe in the midst of dinner. It puts the host on the spot and disrupts the flow of conversation. Some hosts may not like to give away cooking secrets, while others may prefer to share this with you later.

It is no longer taboo to bring up politics or religion in polite conversation, but everyone at the table must exercise self-control and handle the exchange of ideas tactfully. There is nothing better than an honest, lively discussion and nothing worse than an ugly argument to bring the dinner party to a screeching halt. As the host works to make sure her guests are comfortable, so should the guests avoid offending the host and fellow guests. And, as stated in maxim 105 of *George Washington's Rules of Civility and Decent Behavior*: "Be not angry at table whatever happens and if you have reason to be so, show it not but a cheerful countenance, especially if there are strangers, for good humor makes one dish of meat a feast."

II.

Tools of the Table

Cutlery

Knife

The oldest and most important utensil, the knife dates from the Paleolithic era when it was made of flint, ivory, or bone and was used for hunting, cooking, and as a weapon. Its next configuration was the dagger, a pointed knife with a metal blade used for thrusting and stabbing; this was the precursor to the table knife. For many centuries diners brought their own knives, their daggers, to the table, cleaning and sharpening them before entering the great hall. From medieval times the knife was carried in a leather sheath attached to a belt and functioned as a weapon by day and cutlery at night.

For centuries a table setting in most European countries consisted of a knife and spoon that diners brought with them. In sixteenth-century Tudor England, manor houses began to have sets of matching knives to offer guests. Paston-Williams (1993) found that a household inventory of Henry VIII (1491–1547) lists a set of knives decorated with emeralds, amethysts, pearls, even diamonds. Of course, this was not the norm for non-royals.

The ancestor of our modern individual steak knife, the point-ended knife used as cutlery, survived until Cardinal Richelieu, King Louis XIII's chief minister, purportedly rounded the end. Perhaps this was a self-protective move; did he fear courtly intrigues that could be enacted at table? Louis XIV completely redesigned the table knife, giving it a blunted end, and banned pointed knives (hunting daggers) to control violence at table and to keep diners from using the point to clean their teeth! Paston-Williams explains that the rounding of the knife is evolutionary, a consequence of the table fork replacing the knife to spear meat, and the fact that the toothpick, then on the table (yikes!), did a fine job of cleaning teeth.

Many modern rules, really taboos, are based on safety concerns born of rougher times when fights broke out at the banquet table, and one diner stabbed another. Today it is a hard-and-fast rule that the knife is never lifted more than a few inches above table level and never put in the mouth or waved in the air while eating and talking. As an extension of these concerns, in Continental dining both wrists remain on the table in plain view throughout the meal. Concealing one hand in your lap raises questions as to what is going on under the table!

Spoon

The spoon is a small bowl with a handle, also called the stem. Every culture in the world uses the spoon even if chopsticks or human hands are the main utensil. The spoon has been in existence since the late Stone Age when it replaced shells as the scoop for liquids and was carved from stone, wood, or bone to aid cooking and serving. Some examples from this period are beautifully crafted with decorative carvings at the handle's end. In the Middle East and Asia, spoons were used for eating soup as well as for cooking and serving it. The ancient Romans made spoons of bronze and silver designed with slender pointed handles. Medieval spoons with sturdy handles used for cooking and serving were made of affordable materials, wood or bone. In contrast, as early as the thirteenth century, gold and silver service spoons were used by English kings.

Like the evolution of the knife, the shape of the soup bowl and stem evolved and often reflect social and political change. Early seventeenth-century English silver spoons have a fig-shaped bowl that widens at the end that goes in the mouth, and they have a hexagonal stem.

Some stem ends were decorated with sculptural finials including flora, fauna, human, and architectural forms like the souvenir spoons available today. (I have a small collection of nineteenth- and twentieth-century silver souvenir spoons, many with an architectural knop finial.) During the Commonwealth period in the first half of the seventeenth century, the Cromwellian or "Puritan" spoon interpreted the implement stripped to its bare essentials with a shallow egg-shaped bowl and totally plain stem. It was heavy and without a finial, like the decapitated King Charles I. A few years later Charles II's Restoration brought with it a celebration of decoration, including a new spoon shape called the trifid, first hallmarked around 1660. With its deeper, oval bowl and flat handle that flared into three rounded lobes like a clover leaf, a design no doubt inspired by the French fleur-de-lis, it is the prototype for our modern soup and dessert spoons. When the English added sugar and milk to their tea in the seventeenth-century the teaspoon was invented. It is smaller than the trifid and over the centuries has proven to be the most versatile implement used worldwide today.

Fork

Italy of the sixteenth century, most notably Florence and Venice, was the pinnacle of style and refinement. Known for integrating good form and function, Italians introduced the table fork to the European dining room. In existence since the Bronze Age as a two-pronged carving tool, the fork was used in Biblical times, in Roman times (made of silver and bronze), and in the Byzantine Empire by the tenth century, where the carving fork was joined by the table fork.

Venetians brought the table fork from Constantinople to Italy as early as the eleventh century. Fifteenth-century Italian Renaissance paintings document the use of forks in scenes of wedding feasts, although their use was not widespread until the sixteenth century when forks were commonplace in upper-class Italian households. At first guests brought their own spoons, knives, and forks to the table. The Venetian noble lady attached to her belt a cutlery-carrier like the one Patricia Fortini Brown features in her book *Private Lives in Renaissance Venice* (2004). Made of tooled "mosaic" leather, painted and gilded, the carrier has a silk rope handle. Apparently the cutlery was more rarefied than the carrier, like the gold mid-sixteenth-century knife-fork-spoon set with faceted crystal handles that I recently saw at Museo Correr in Venice.

Catherine de' Medici introduced the fork to the court of France. As the new bride of Henri II, she arrived in Paris in 1533 with her *cadena*, a small decorative box containing her personal fork and knife set—the custom among nobles in Florence. Shortly afterward she insisted that a complete set of cutlery be provided for each of her dinner guests at court. Catherine is also credited with bringing to the royal French banquet table Italian *haute cuisine* as well as ice cream, artichokes, melons, broccoli, cabbage; meals served in courses; and table manners.

Italians were mocked and labeled effeminate for the practice of using forks, never mind that eating this way promoted cleanliness and cut down on laundering the all-important napkin (towel) needed to mop up after supper. Italians were, once again, way ahead of their time. Until the Italians introduced Europeans to the table fork, it was used only by royalty and the well-to-do; then, trickling down the social class ladder over hundreds of years, it became standard equipment. The Italians also introduced to the table the serving spoon.

The English insisted on eating with their hands, which put their table manners a century behind the Italians. Although a set of tiny, bejeweled forks used only for eating sweetmeats was found in the household inventory of Henry VIII (middle sixteenth century), the fork did not take hold in England until the seventeenth century. Paston-Williams credits "the eccentric traveler" Thomas Coryat with introducing the fork into English society. The author of *Coryat's Crudities* (1611) wrote about his experiences on the Continent: "The Italians do always at their meals, use a little fork, when they cut their meat. For with their knife, which they hold in one hand, they cut the meat out of the dish, they fasten their fork, which they hold in their other hand upon the same dish." Paston-Williams writes that as late as 1669, foreign visitors to England complained about the absence of forks and that diners were still expected to bring their own knife and spoon, the only items of cutlery used widely.

The knife, fork, and spoon all rose to prominence and widespread use during the industrial revolution, which began in the middle eighteenth century and continued through the nineteenth century. The thriving cutlery industry in Sheffield, England, improved manufacturing and commercialism in America made these symbols of refinement accessible. In the mid to late nineteenth century the gradual move from *service à la française* (all the dishes placed on the table at once) to *service à la russe* (dinner served in successive courses with specific utensils for each course) gave rise to all the finicky variations of the table knife, fork, and spoon. Each pattern is named and has its own style that interprets subtly (or not so subtly) the shape of the knife or the number of prongs on the fork. We still use a two-pronged carving fork. In some vintage patterns you may see a ham fork with prongs that distinguish it from the hot meat fork, different from the cold meat fork, all shapes and sizes mostly for serving. A three-pronged or four-pronged table fork of different sizes for lunch and dinner may appear on the table with the fish fork, with its distinctive pointed tip and widened left prong. The fish fork is not the same as the dainty oyster fork or the crab fork, which may be called a generic cocktail fork. A salad fork is similar to a dessert fork but smaller than the luncheon fork, not to be confused with the pickle fork or fruit fork. The list is dizzying for sure, and reciting the many variations sounds like Bubba's unforgettable and incredibly droll shrimp monologue from the movie *Forrest Gump*! Then we have the oval soup spoon, the round bouillon spoon, the cereal spoon, the teaspoon, the demi-tasse spoon, the tiny flat sorbet spoon, the double-ended marrow spoon, the flat potato chip spoon, the fluted berry spoon, and the grapefruit spoon...

cocktail fork, salad fork, luncheon fork, dinner fork, dinner knife, luncheon knife, butter knife/spreader, bouillon spoon, table/soup spoon, dessert/cereal spoon, grapefruit/fruit spoon, teaspoon

With every passing day our modern world becomes more informal, and it is no longer necessary to know every quaint variation in cutlery. What is necessary is to know how to set the table; how to recognize which utensil to use with each course; and most important, how to properly hold the knife, fork, and spoon.

The arrangement of cutlery at the place setting has changed little in two hundred years. Cutlery is arranged in the order of use. Knives and spoons are placed on the right side of the plate, forks on the left, except in the case of a cocktail fork, which may rest in the bowl of the soup spoon. You will start from the outside and work your way in for each course. At the top of the place setting there is often a fork with prongs pointing right and a dessert spoon, its bowl facing left, that are used for the dessert course. Please note that *only* dessert cutlery rests at the top of the plate. If you are setting your own table, pay strict attention to this rule; otherwise you confuse your guests. (See "Dessert Course" in chapter 3.)

Occasionally, yet very rarely, cutlery is mistakenly and incorrectly arranged according to size, starting with the smallest utensil on the outside and the largest ones nearest the plate. This can be very confusing. In this instance the diner must know the shape and size of the utensils in order to select the correct one for the course presented. If you aren't sure of what is going on, watch someone who does know. And if you make a mistake, just keep going; don't look around in a panic.

After identifying the cutlery, the next step is learning how to properly hold it. This is very important, so pay close attention. The knife is always used by the right hand. To hold the knife, rest the handle in the palm of your hand. The thumb and index finger secure the knife. The thumb runs down the inside of the handle and the index finger on the back. The hand never touches the blade, and it is bad form to choke the handle, which means holding it too close to the blade. The fork may be held in the right hand or the left hand. If in the right hand, hold the fork as you would a pencil; it rests on the middle finger, steadied by the index finger and secured by the thumb. In this position the prongs are always up.

When the fork is used in conjunction with the knife for cutting, or in the Continental style to push food with the knife onto the back of the fork, move the fork to the left hand. The prongs are *always* down. In this position the fork is held like the knife. Rest the handle, or part of it, in the palm of your hand. The index finger runs down the top of the fork and the thumb steadies it. Remember: don't put a choke hold on the fork, either, and *never* hold it perpendicular to the plate even when cutting (See "Meat Course" in chapter 3).

Hold the spoon the same way you hold the fork when in the right hand, like a pen or pencil. Hold it near the end of the spoon, as with the fork and knife, to avoid gripping near the bowl (which is another way of saying, don't do the choke hold; it looks clumsy).

American and Continental Styles

There are two styles of eating with forks and knives: American and Continental. Both are correct, but the Continental style is widely used all over the world. You cannot go wrong learning the Continental method, especially if, for school, for work, or for pleasure, international travel is in your future. In my opinion, adopting the Continental method of eating is not only practical but diplomatic: one small gesture quietly counters the sense of cultural arrogance communicated by many Americans.

In his book *In Small Things Forgotten: An Archaeology of Early American Life*, James Deetz does not remark on which hand holds the fork but explains why Americans turn the prongs up. "Americans often comment that Europeans use their forks 'upside down.' In fact, by the simple rule of priority and majority, it is we Americans who are 'upside down.' Since we did not learn to use forks until some time after the ends of knives were rounded, the change in the manner of food conveyance was not directly from knife tip to fork tine, as it was in England. The only immediate utensil was the spoon; one could cut food and transfer it to the spoon bowl. If even one generation used knife and spoon in this manner, the fork, upon its belated appearance, would be used in a manner similar to the spoon. Which is precisely the way we use it today... This distinctive way of using the knife, fork, and spoon came into existence during the late seventeenth and early eighteenth centuries, and thus is one more American idiosyncrasy arising from isolation during that period."

Emily Post, in *Etiquette*, says that no one really knows how the American style began and advocates for the "expert way" that we call Continental style. She has this to say about the "zigzag" or American way of eating:

> The procedure called zigzag eating is this: With the knife in right hand and fork in left, the diner cuts a piece of meat. Then instead of lifting the piece to the mouth with fork in left hand—or at least cutting

several pieces—the knife is laid down, the fork transferred to right hand, turned over, tines up [left hand dropped out of sight to the diner's lap], and the meat speared and conveyed to the mouth. Then the fork is zigzagged back into the left hand and turned over, tines down, while the knife is picked up again and another piece of food cut. Again the knife is laid down, fork turned over and zigzagged to the right hand—don't let us even picture it. The only serious objection to making the right hand do all the work is that no form of limping, whether it be of foot or hand, expresses effortless ease. And why an able-bodied person should like to pretend that the left hand is paralyzed and cannot be lifted more than three or four inches above the table is beyond understanding.

Many prominent etiquette books discuss no other way of eating than the Continental style because it is simpler, more practical, and streamlined. Walter Hoving's *Tiffany's Table Manners for Teenagers* discourages the American style: "After cutting the meat, never place the knife across the corner of the plate. Don't keep shifting the fork from the left to the right hand. This is clumsy and awkward."

With the Continental method the fork is in the left hand. The prongs are *always* pointing down when the fork is held in the left hand. The knife is in the right hand and is used for cutting and pushing food onto the back of the fork, which delivers the food to the mouth with a slight lift of the forearm and rotation of the wrist. The diner holds the fork in the left hand and the knife in the right throughout the meal, unless, of course, he or she chooses to use only the fork for salad, rice, or soft fish. Elbows stay close to the body, forearms may rest on the table; and when you need to pause and take a sip of water or wipe your mouth with the napkin, do not leave the utensils hanging off the edge of the plate like oars on a boat. Leave them in "rest" position with the fork, prongs down, crossed over the knife with its blade turned in. This says that you are still eating.

When you finish the course, place the fork and knife together on the right side of the plate at approximately 5 o'clock. (Beware that the British say "finished" position is at six-thirty!) In this position the fork, prongs up or down, is on the left and the knife is on the right, the blade turned towards the fork. (The British say that the fork prongs are always down.) Remember these two positions whenever fork and knife are employed. (See "Fish Course," "Meat Course," and "Salad Course" in chapter 3.)

Rest   *Finished*

If you must put down the knife after cutting and eat with the fork alone, rest the knife on the upper right side of the plate with the blade facing in. "Rest" and "finished" are the same for both the Continental and American ways of eating.

Whether you choose the Continental or the American zigzag style of eating, the goal is to get the food into your mouth without drawing attention to yourself.

Napkins

You will find the napkin folded and placed in the center of the service plate (and that is the *only* time your napkin is allowed in your plate!), resting directly on the table between the knives and forks, or to the left of the forks. Once you are seated, pick up your napkin, unfold it, and place it in your lap. If it is a very large napkin, leave it folded in half, the folded edge closest to you.

If you have to leave the table temporarily, fold the napkin loosely and put it to the left of the plate, which also signals to waiters that you will be back.

At the end of the meal, do not refold the napkin as if never used. Instead, fold it loosely and put it to the left of the place setting. *Do not* under any circumstances ball up the cloth napkin and throw it into the dirty dinner plate as one guest did at my house recently (and we still had the dessert course ahead of us)! Do not use the napkin to wipe your sweating face, blow your nose, or clean your teeth or the cutlery.

Regarding that last bit of advice, many agree that it is acceptable to tap the nose with the napkin, but if you have a sudden need to delicately blow your nose, as in a sneeze, do it quickly and quietly using your handkerchief if you have one. To be really polite, excuse yourself from the table to take care of serious nose-blowing.

The Table Setting

The formal setting pictured below is for six courses. See if you can "read" the table setting to identify the courses.

As indicated by the pictured arrangement of cutlery, the first course will be oysters, crab, or shrimp cocktail eaten with the tiny eponymous fork you see resting in the bowl of the soup spoon. This is the traditional placement, although one might occasionally find the cocktail fork to the far left of the dinner and salad forks if the fish course is omitted (there should never be more than three forks and three knives on either side of the plate). The second course will be soup; the third course will be fish followed by the fourth course, meat; then salad is fifth; and dessert is sixth. Some refer to the arrival of coffee as a course, but it is not one. If there is a sorbet course (which would make a total of seven courses), it is placed on the table after the fish course, and in this case there is no sorbet spoon in the setting because the dish and small spoon are served together.

After each course glasses as well as the cutlery accompanying the course are removed. That is the formal rule, at least. At less formal catered business and university dinners, waiters leave various glasses on the table to satisfy diners who prefer red over white wine and vice versa.

champagne, water, red wine, white wine, claret or sherry

Before dessert is served, all the plates and unused cutlery from previous courses must be removed, as well as the salt and pepper, condiments, and so forth. Once the table is cleared a well-trained waiter will crumb the table. Only the dessert fork, dessert spoon, champagne flute (or dessert wine glass), and water goblet remain. If coffee is served at the table the dessert wine glass stays through coffee.

III.

The Formal Dinner

Seating

When all the guests have arrived at the table, make sure that you have met everyone. Introduce yourself and shake hands, but remain standing. Wait for the host to explain his or her seating plan by saying, "So-and-so, please sit here," or to invite the guests to identify their place cards. *Never* move place cards around so that you may sit with a friend or in a certain location. This rule is set in stone. The host has given thoughtful consideration to who should sit with whom.

A traditional seating arrangement alternates men and women. If the host is a man, the female guest of honor is to his right; the hostess seats the male guest of honor to her right. In social situations it is expected that gentlemen pull out chairs for ladies. (The old-school rule says that a lady looks to the man on the left to help her with the chair, but today she appreciates this courtesy regardless of its coming from right or left.) He holds the chair as she moves to its right side and sits down while he pushes the chair in. The modern woman, however, does not mind seating herself and may do so especially if she arrives at table before her dinner partner. Like holding the door for the next person regardless of gender, everyone at the table should be attentive to the seating of the elderly or handicapped guest. Men remain standing until all of the ladies are seated and until the hostess sits down. Guests may sit down only when the host gestures or says, "Please be seated." Put the napkin in your lap when the host picks up his or hers. This small move begins the subtle, unspoken choreography of a dinner party or business meal.

Seating protocol gets confusing when the fine line between business and purely social functions blurs. At professional breakfasts, lunches, and dinners, rank supersedes gender and some women feel patronized by a man holding the chair for them. Gentlemen, perhaps the best advice is that in a purely business setting you ask permission to pull out her chair and seat her. "May I help you?" is the best tactic for bridging both worlds. Although such chivalrous gestures are not always necessary, they are much appreciated.

Once you are seated remember the power of posture. Don't slump or drape your arm over the chair back. Sit up straight, but lean toward the table as you eat. An important concept to remember is that your chair and the place setting in front of you define your space. This is like the frame when you are dancing. Reaching across your dinner partner is rude, like a driver who cuts you off at an intersection, and you may be inviting danger. You may knock over a glass or interrupt a bite midway from plate to mouth. For goodness sake, don't stand up and reach across the table for salt and pepper, a condiment, or to refill another's water or wine glass as one tall guest gripping a red wine bottle did at my table! Ask for things out of reach to be passed to you, but do not ever get up and walk to the other end of the table to fetch something you want.

One last word about seating: NEVER lean back in the chair. How many times have you heard this? Between courses it is perfectly polite to rest your torso against the chair back, but do not push back in the chair balancing on its rear legs. Not long ago at a small but formal seated dinner party, the man next to me leaned back in his chair. When I heard a cracking noise, I turned to see what was happening and quietly warn him about the alarming sound. The chair came apart and the man fell to the floor. The upper section of the chair broke off entirely, flipped in the air, and hit him on the head. He was out cold for a few minutes, and EMS declared him injured but not seriously. That is not the bang-up ending you want for your party!

Service

You should always be served food on your left side. Below I provide a helpful little memory trick that is useful if you are being served by waiters—and we pray that they know what they are doing—or if you are asked to help serve and remove plates at an informal dinner.

At large catered dinners, plates are prepared in the kitchen, and if the waiters are well trained they know to arrive at your left side to place yours in front of you. In upscale restaurants or at formal dinner parties the waiter may bring a platter to your left side and ask if he or she may serve you this course. At smaller formal dinner parties the server comes to the left side of each guest with a platter from which guests may serve themselves for the fish course and again for the meat course. A serving fork and spoon rest on the side of the platter. Hold the fork in the left hand and the spoon in the right hand to serve yourself. When finished, place the serving fork and spoon together at the right side of the platter. Take small portions and feel free to refuse something you don't care for, but do it quietly with a simple, "No, thank you," and certainly without a long explanation about your being vegetarian or allergic. To avoid offending the host, put something on your plate to look as if you are eating. When second helpings are offered, take them or say, "No, thank you; I have had enough." Don't announce, "I'm done," or even worse, "I'm stuffed" or "I'm full" and pat your stomach. "I'm full" in French means "I'm pregnant!"

If you do not drink alcoholic beverages, when wine is offered simply touch the rim of the glass and say, "No, thank you." Do not turn the glass upside down or make a scene, and if wine is poured into your glass by mistake, simply ignore it.

When plates are removed at the end of the course they will be removed from your right side. Here is the memory device: lower (food) left, raise (food) right. All beverages are served *and* removed from the right. If the dinner is informal and guests help remove the plates after each course, remove them from the right and take only two plates at a time, one in each hand. Scrape and stack plates in the kitchen, never at the table.

When there is no wait staff, the host passes the platter in a counter-clockwise direction by turning first to the guest of honor seated to his right and placing the platter on the table at the guest's left; or the host holds the platter so that the guest may serve himself. The guest then passes it to the person on the right. Again, the reason for the counter-clockwise direction for passing is so that all guests receive their food from the left. It is always thoughtful to offer to hold the platter for the next person. Remember, pass to the right.

When asked to pass a bowl or the salt and pepper, put the object on the table for the next person to use or pass along, but *do not* exchange things midair! And always pass the salt and pepper together, even if a dinner companion asks only for salt.

In a large group at a banquet or in a ballroom with many round tables where the service time is long and the food may get cold, it is perfectly correct to begin without waiting for everyone to be served. Don't dive into your plate, though; wait until three or four people at your table have received their food, as this demonstrates restraint and social awareness. In a smaller setting, especially a private dinner party at home, begin eating when the host picks up her fork and knife or when she says, "Please, go ahead and begin without me." At the end of the meal when coffee is offered, don't turn the cup upside down on the saucer if you do not care for any. It is distracting. When the server comes to you, just say, "No, thank you."

Bread and Butter

Bite not thy bread and lay it down,
That is no curtesy to use in town.
—*The Boke of Curtesye*, ca. 1350

Small hard rolls are traditionally wrapped in the linen dinner napkin and placed on the service plate or directly on the table in the middle of the place setting. Sometimes they sit directly on the tablecloth.

Individual plates for bread and butter are often called simply "butter plates," not to be confused with the communal butter service dish. Individual butter plates are always accompanied by individual butter knives that rest on the side of the plate. However, this tiny bread and butter plate and knife are not always a part of the table setting.

If butter is passed, cut a small portion of butter from the butter dish with the service knife provided, and put your slice of butter on your own butter plate, which should be located at the top left above the forks. If there is no butter plate, put the slice of butter on your dinner plate. Use your own butter knife to spread the butter and not the one that you have just used from the butter service.

Never use your knife to cut bread. Use your fingers to break off a piece of bread, butter just that one bite, not the entire roll, and using your *left* hand, eat the bite of bread. At a private dinner party if butter is not served, as in the case of a baguette at less formal occasions, it is impolite to ask for it or, for that matter, any other condiments for dipping bread.

At a formal dinner do not use bread as a pusher or to sop up juices or sauces on your plate. In informal dining situations it is acceptable to use a small piece of bread like this: discreetly break a bit off the bread or roll, drop it into your plate, stab it with the fork (left hand, prongs down) and use your knife in the right hand (as a pusher) to absorb the remaining sauce. Here is what Giovanni Della Casa had to say about it in 1558: "A well-mannered man must therefore take heed not to smear his fingers so much that his napkin is left soiled, for it is disgusting to see. And even wiping one's fingers on the bread one is about to eat does not seem a polite habit" (Della Casa 1986).

Soup Course

> And when your potage you shall be brouhte, take your sponys and soupe by no way, and in you're dysshe leve not your spone, I pray.—*The Babees Book of Manners*, 1475

Traditionally, the soup is served in a soup plate at dinner and in a soup cup with two handles at lunch when serving cream soups or bouillon. Today, both bowl styles are used interchangeably, but the soup plate is still preferred for formal dinners.

The bowl of the soup spoon may be round or oval, although the British regard the round bouillon spoon as *déclassé*, a bourgeois invention. The oval-bowled soup spoon is most common and versatile.

The soup spoon is held in the right hand. It is steadied between the index finger and middle fingers with the thumb on top, as the fork is held in the right hand. Fill the soup spoon by moving it away from you. There is some disagreement about sipping from the side of the spoon versus sipping from the end. Sipping from the side is generally regarded as more polite. However, some thick soups—soups with chopped vegetables or bits of fish or meat—are difficult to eat this way; discreetly eat them from the end of the spoon. (British etiquette writers warn that turning the spoon at a right angle to the mouth is bad form.) Sip from the side or eat from the end, but always silently. No slurping noises! Don't blow on a spoonful of hot soup (or any other food for that matter) to cool it before eating. "Where there is wind there is rain," wrote

Giovanni Della Casa in *Il Galateo*! If you take a bite of something that is hot, quietly take a sip of water, and never spit out hot food. If needed, sip water again.

As you finish the last of the soup it is all right to tip the plate away from you, but just slightly. While resting or when finished, leave the spoon in the soup plate or on the side of the under plate if there is room.

soup plate: rest (left) and finished (right)

If the soup is served in a cup with two handles, it may be eaten with a spoon or by lifting the cup by the handles to drink directly. This is the *only* time it is acceptable to pick up a soup bowl! While resting between sips or when finished, you may place the spoon on the service plate. Never leave the spoon in the bowl.

soup bowl: rest and finished

Fish Course

If fish is served as a separate course before the meat or poultry course, the fish will be the only thing on the plate. For formal private dinners and in the fanciest restaurants it is customary to provide a fish knife and fish fork. Use both of them for this course.

In case the cutlery is arranged by size from smallest to largest, and not by the order of the courses, it is important to recognize the shape of the fish knife and fish fork and how they differ from the luncheon and dinner forks and knives. If a fish knife and fish fork are not included in the utensils on either side of the dinner plate, use the smaller knives and forks.

The fork is held in the left hand, prongs down. The fish knife is used to cut and push. The off-center tapered point is to de-bone if the fish is served whole. The fish knife is held differently from the meat knife. Hold it like a pencil or a fork. The index finger and thumb are on top and the middle finger acts as a support beneath.

The fish knife and fish fork should be held like this

To remove the flesh from the bone, use both the knife and fork starting at the head of the fish to extricate one bite at a time. Move along the spine to the tail, and don't flip Mr. Fish or make a big production of de-boning like a fishmonger to remove the skeleton. Work with your knife and fork to secure little bites from beneath. This is completely doable. If you get a bone by accident, place the fork and knife in "rest" position and discreetly spit it into the cupped left hand or use your two fingers to remove it and place it delicately on the side of the plate.

If the fish is soft and already boned, you may choose to leave the knife on the table and use only the fork. When you are finished place the fork, prongs down, next to the knife, whether it has been used or not, in "finished" position. This signals the waiter that you have completed the fish course.

Meat Course

Hold the meat or dinner knife in your right hand with the forefinger pointing down the knife, thumb on the side. The meat knife is held differently from the fish knife. Hold the fork in the left hand, prongs down. When held in the left hand the prongs of the fork always point down. Forearms may rest on the table. This position does not change in the Continental style, which is more practical and elegant. As mentioned earlier, shifting the knife and fork back and forth after cutting is the American style, also known as "zigzag eating." You are free to choose either method, but observe some basic points. Throughout the meal, elbows stay close to the body in a relaxed way, not clinching. Resting your elbows on the table between courses and at the end of the meal is perfectly acceptable.

To cut meat one holds the utensils the same way for both Continental and American styles. Hold the knife in your right hand with the forefinger pointing down the knife, and the fork in the left hand, prongs down.

The dinner knife and fork should be held like this

When you exert pressure in cutting, do not lift your elbows as if you are a bird taking flight!

Don't

Never stab the meat while holding the fork perpendicular to the plate and don't grip it with your fist. Never hold the knife in the left hand.

Don't

Don't hold the cutlery with fists for any reason. It looks crude and hostile.

Don't

Do not cut all your meat at once as if preparing a dinner plate for a small child; cut one piece of meat at a time. After you have eaten a bite, cut the next. But do cut the meat. (I heard about a young woman who was served a T-bone steak at dinner and because it had a bone, as does fried chicken, she picked up the whole steak in her hands and bit off a piece, Hungry Man style!)

If you get a bite of gristle, remove it on the prongs of your fork and place it on the edge of the plate; or spit the seeds, pits, or shot from fowl or other game meat into the cupped left hand without anyone noticing and place it on the edge of the plate. In an emergency, use your fingers to remove gristle, seeds, and bones by discreetly putting your thumb and index finger in your mouth to remove the object, and again, place it on the edge of the plate.

Never gesture with your fork or knife.

Don't

"It is perfectly proper to talk with the fork and knife in your hands but do not gesticulate with the fork and knife," Hoving warns. "The knife should never be raised more than an inch or two above the plate. If you remember this rule you will never be caught with your knife in your mouth."

Although Emily Post says that using your knife as a pusher to shovel food onto the fork, prongs up, is acceptable, the prevailing opinion is that this is bad form, and I agree. To be safe, keep the prongs down. As Hoving writes, "Never hold the fork in the left hand with prongs up and pile food on it with the knife. Never hold the knife in the left hand." You may use the knife in the right hand as a pusher and combine vegetables and potatoes on the *back* of the fork—prongs down.

Don't encircle the plate with your left hand while you eat with the right hand.

Don't

Do not hold the fork or knife with one hand while simultaneously wiping your mouth or drinking from a glass.

Don't

When you need to take a sip of wine or water, eat a piece of bread, or use your napkin, do not leave your utensils hanging off the edge of the plate to rest on the table.

Don't

The rule is that once you have used your cutlery, it never again touches the table. Instead, place the utensils on the plate in "rest" position with the knife and fork crossed, the fork prongs facing down to cross over the knife blade that is turned in.

Sadly, waiters are not always well trained and do not understand the "resting" and "finished" positions and may try to remove your plate when you are just pausing. In this case, politely say that you are not finished. When you have completed the course, place the fork and knife together on the right side of the plate at approximately 5 o'clock.

Rest   *Finished*

Salad Course

For the salad course, the knife and fork may be used the same way as for the fish and meat courses. Hold the knife in your right hand and the fork in your left hand. Use the knife to push and to cut large, unwieldy lettuce leaves or other components of a less traditional salad (for example, tomatoes, artichoke hearts) that are too big to eat in one bite. If you wish, you may simply cut the lettuce with the edge of the fork. Guidelines for cutting and eating salad are the same as for both meat and fish: don't use your knife and fork to cut up the entire plate of salad at once, as if preparing the plate for a child. If the salad is served with meat at lunch you can use the same fork for both.

The same rules for "rest" and "finished" apply to the salad course. Even if you have used only the fork for the salad course, it is always a good idea to put the salad knife and salad fork together on the plate at 5 o'clock to signal the staff that you have finished.

Finger Bowl

Sometimes after enjoying messy finger food, or at very formal dinners regardless of the menu, a finger bowl precedes the dessert course. The finger bowl is made of silver or glass filled with tepid water. In restaurants it may be presented with a lemon slice or a flower floating on top. The bowl rests on a cloth doily placed on the dessert plate and is accompanied by a fork on the left side of the plate and spoon on the right. When the server places the bowl in front of you, remove the fork and spoon to place them to the left and right of your dessert plate respectively.

Pick up the doily and the finger bowl together. Place them in front of you to the left above the fork at 11 o'clock.

If the finger bowl is presented *after* dessert there will be no fork and spoon and the bowl and under plate remain in front of you. Dip your fingers in the water one hand at a time and gently pat your hands with your napkin. With minimal fanfare, place the napkin back in your lap.

Don't push the dishes away from you when you have finished dessert or finished using the finger bowl. And don't say, "I'm finished" and push your chair back from the table. However, when the dinner is over and everyone lingers in conversation, it is perfectly polite to relax into the chair and give yourself more room to cross your legs.

Dessert Course

Americans call the last course dessert; the French say *désert* (day-zair). The British say *pudding* when they are referring to a sweet ending and *dessert* when it is fruit. The Italians call it *dolce*, and the Germans say *nachtisch*, *nachspeise*, or just plain *dessert*. Whatever you call it, it is always a welcomed treat.

When the dessert is served and the plate placed before you, take the fork and dessert spoon from the top of your place setting and put them on the table to the sides of your dessert plate, the spoon on the right and the fork on the left. Bring the spoon to the right side of the plate and the fork to the left.

Hold the fork in the left hand with the prongs down and the spoon in the right hand. Eat with the spoon and push with the fork, or use the fork to anchor tricky frozen desserts or pies and tarts with crusts too dense to cut with the edge of a fork and that might scoot off the plate if you try to eat them with a spoon alone. If the dessert is a delicate custard, such as *crème caramel* or chocolate mousse, use only the spoon; for soft cake you may use only the fork. But if ice cream and cake are served, use both the spoon and fork as described above.

Sometimes fruit is served instead of sweets. The old-fashioned formal way to eat fruit, especially a whole orange, apple, or pear, is with the knife and fork, not the hands, although some now mock this method. It takes practice; try it at home before you tackle the challenge in public.

Grapes are always pinched off in small bunches with your hands or cut off with grape shears. *Never* pluck one grape at a time; this is very rude. Cherries are eaten whole, the seeds spat into the left hand and placed on the side of the plate as you would fish bones, gristle, and shot, or discreetly use two fingers to extract the seed.

Quarter figs with knife and fork, then eat each section with the hands, leaving stem and any unwanted skin on the side of the plate.

At the dinner table never pick up a banana, peel it, and eat it like a monkey swinging from trees in the jungle! Use your knife to peel it in long strips, then use your knife to cut small bites one at a time, or use the knife to cut small pieces to eat with a fork or your fingers.

According to *DeBrett's* (Morgan 1996), the modern way to eat apples, pears, and oranges permits the use of your hands. Hold the apple in the left hand and the knife in the right hand to remove sections of peeling. Once free of all peeling cut the apple in sections and eat with the hand. Do the same with pears, although I would quarter the unpeeled fruit and use a knife and fork to cut smaller bites.

Why anyone would want to eat a whole, juicy orange for dessert at the dinner table is beyond me. But if you so choose, hold the orange in the left hand and the knife in the right hand to remove the skin in one piece circling the fruit or in sections as with apples and pears. Eat the orange sections by hand or, as I would, with a knife and fork because it is so messy. Peel and eat clementines, tangerines, and other citrus with your hands.

For dessert the "rest" position is with the spoon on the right and the fork, prongs down, crossed over the spoon just like the knife and fork in other courses.

rest   *finished*

The "finished" position is with the spoon facing up and the fork prongs up or down. Put both on the plate at 5 o'clock, even if you have used only one of them. This signals to the staff to remove your service or to your hostess that you have finished.

Coffee

Coffee and tea may be served with dessert or after dessert when dishes from all previous courses have been removed from the table. (It can come on its own the same way after-dinner drinks are served at the table, but it is not a course.) Remember, don't drink coffee with the spoon in the cup. If you are offered tea instead, remove the tea bag and the spoon from the cup before drinking.

Leaving the Table

When your host puts his or her napkin on the table and stands, it is a signal for all that the dinner is over. Do not leave the table until then. Loosely fold the napkin; never crumple or, even worse, wad it up and throw it into the plate.

Place it to the left of the dessert plate, or coffee cup if there is no plate, and slowly rise from your chair. Gentlemen, if you want to exhibit traditional good manners, let the ladies exit the dining room first.

IV.

A Review

Do's

Do turn off cell phones and other electronics, including cameras, before entering the dining room, and store them out of sight.

Do wait for the host's signal to be seated, to begin eating, and to leave the table.

Do sit at the table with good posture, and minimize wiggling and gesturing.

Do ask for a replacement instead of reaching for cutlery that has fallen on the floor.

Do take small bites; eat slowly enough to carry on a conversation.

Do chew with your mouth closed.

Do ask that salt and pepper be passed to you; never reach for things on the table.

Do leave the fork and knife in "rest" position (never hanging off the plate) when you need to pause, take a sip of water or wine, or leave the table for a moment.

Do leave the fork and knife in "finished" position when you have finished the course.

Do wait until the last person has finished eating before removing the plates.

Do order things that are easy to eat; big sloppy salads and spaghetti are obvious problems.

Don'ts

Don't *ever* move place cards so that you may sit with a friend or in a certain spot; if you see someone doing this, quietly return the place card to its original position.

Don't sit down in a restaurant until invited to do so by the host (the same applies in an office, especially if you are there for an interview); stand until you are invited to sit.

Don't order an alcoholic drink at a business lunch or dinner if the host does not order one, and have only *one* drink in any circumstance; if you are first to order, play it safe and order a soft drink.

Don't lift the soup bowl (or a bowl of anything, for that matter) close to your face to spoon soup into your mouth; always leave the soup bowl or soup plate on the table (see the "Soup Course" section above).

Don't clean the silverware with your napkin.

Don't drink coffee with the spoon in the cup or tea with the tea bag in the cup.

Don't stuff your mouth with food and then try to talk.

Don't smack or slurp while eating.

Don't sample food or drink and then make smacking noises as if to say, "I'm tasting it."

Don't wash down your food with wine or water.

Don't lick the knife!

Don't gesture with utensils, as common as it is in all senses of the word.

Don't blow on hot food to cool it before taking a bite.

Don't spit out hot food; quietly take a sip of water, then another if needed.

Don't announce, "I'm stuffed" or "I'm full" (or even pat your stomach).

Don't push the plate away declaring, "I'm through," pat your stomach, throw the cloth napkin in your plate, then push your chair back from the table—like a pig leaving the trough.

Don't *ever* ball up, wad, or gently place your cloth napkin in your plate.

Don't blow your nose with the host's cloth napkin.

Don't yawn and stretch or scratch yourself at the table.

"Don't touch your head at the table,"Johnson writes, and certainly don't touch a friend's head or reach over and adjust his or her hair!

Don't lean back in the chair (see the broken chair story).

Don't use a toothpick at the table or anywhere other than in private.

A Few Finger Foods and Foods Difficult to Eat

Asparagus is always a finger food in Europe, where you may (rarely) be presented with asparagus tongs, and also in some American circles. Eat asparagus with the left hand. Some advise using the fork in the right hand to cut off a bit of the stalk, then picking up the shortened piece with your fingers. It is also polite to use your fork and knife as usual to make small bites, especially if the stalk is too long and droopy or if it is dripping in sauce.

Artichoke is a finger food in America. Each leaf is pulled off one at a time and just the soft, fleshy tips are scraped discreetly between the teeth. Most Europeans throw away the leaves and cook only the heart, which one eats with fork and knife.

Corn on the cob is often served for dinner in America, but never at formal occasions. Hold the ends in your hand and politely bite the kernels.

Fried chicken, especially southern fried chicken, is a finger food at a picnic or barbecue. If it is served at the dinner table, it is cut like all other meats using fork and knife.

Lobster is a finger food but so difficult to eat that it requires special tools, a bib, and a warm wash cloth to clean hands and face afterward.

In the sense that one holds the shell in one hand and uses a fork to retrieve the goodies inside, **mussels** are a finger food, along with **oysters on the half shell** and some crustaceans. But they are rarely presented at a formal occasion. **Shrimp cocktail** may at times be a finger food, unless it is served with a cocktail fork.

The very polite way to eat **pizza** is with a knife and fork, not the hands. **Open-face sandwiches** require the use of fork and knife.

Spaghetti is eaten with a fork. Stab a bit of spaghetti and turn the fork around and around pressing against the plate or the side of the bowl until the pasta forms a tidy bite. Never use a tablespoon or knife. Pasta in general is a fork food.

Illustrations of Table Settings

A Formal Dinner in Six Courses

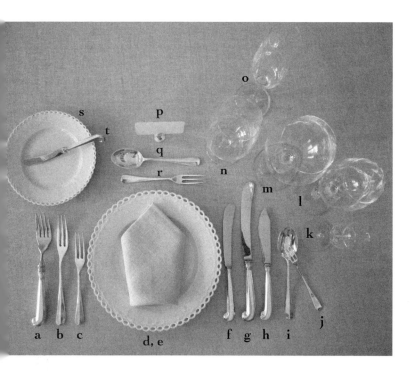

a. fish fork
b. dinner fork
c. salad fork
d. place plate
e. napkin
f. salad knife
g. dinner knife
h. fish knife
i. soup spoon
j. cocktail fork

k. sherry glass
l. white wine glass
m. red wine glass
n. water goblet
o. champagne flute
p. place card
q. dessert spoon
r. dessert fork
s. bread and butter plate
t. butter knife/spreader

A Formal Dinner in Five Courses

A Less Formal Meal in Four Courses

V.

A Brief History of Courtesy and Table Manners

The picayune details of etiquette go in and out of style or come full circle as clothing styles do, but the underlying principles of courtesy are a constant. "Style is the dress of thought," wrote Lord Chesterfield to his son in 1749. *How* a person dresses, walks, talks, writes, dances, eats is his or her style—a kind of language, really. And the mode of execution speaks volumes.

The word *dress* in the quote above alludes to many things. It can mean outer clothing, outward form; and as a verb it means to set in order or put straight. We dress a person, a turkey, a wound, a theater, a store window. But some of us forget to dress our thoughts, especially at the table. In the South we have an expression, "put on your Sunday-best manners," meaning, put your best foot forward. You may recall that Shakespeare wrote "apparel oft proclaims the man," or in modern English, "clothes make the man." Mark Twain also quipped, "Clothes make the man. Naked people have little or no influence in society."

How we dress reveals how we see our society and our own place in it. Plato (429–347 B.C.) noted that a gentleman knows how to throw his cloak from left to right, and never extends his arm outside his *himation* (mantle) or wears his *chiton* (tunic) so short that his knees stick out when he sits down. Of course, grace, variety, and distinction are achieved by the skill of the wearer. Thus the eccentric Socrates (469–399 B.C.) wore only his *himation* draped about him, with nothing under it, to show economy and endurance against the elements. It is worth noting that although the Greeks admired and celebrated the beauty of the human body, women could not appear in public without both *chiton* and *himation*. The style was a demand not for modesty but for decorum, an aesthetic demand.

The Romans were copycats when it came to dress. Their costume was at first an imitation of the Greeks, until they added the toga as an emblem of Roman citizenship—for men only. Less about grace and individual style, the toga was important to the ancient Romans because it defined and restricted specific styles to make rank and social class immediately recognizable in codified dress. Two examples of the many variations are the simple off-white *toga virilis* designated for all citizens over the age of sixteen, and the emperor's Tyrian purple *toga picta*, grandly draped and with elaborate gold borders, symbolizing exclusivity and the authority and power of its wearer. Our modern military uniforms likewise come in various colors and with stripes and insignias that announce rank: the power colors and abundant decoration worn by "top brass" command respect. Although devoid of stars and stripes, the conservative business suit also projects reliability and power. And it provides psychological protection, as it reconfirms to the wearer his achievement and professionalism—his self-image as a player in his particular society.

Medieval Manners: Fanfare and Filth

Greek and Roman sculpture documents the dress of these ancient people, while art and literature depict their customs. Edith Rickert, in her introduction to her modern translation of *The Babees' Book*, writes that the earliest works allude to an elaborate system of manners that guided behavior long before it was codified. She points to the Bayeux Tapestry (A.D. 1073–83), 230 feet of embroidered linen that tell the story surrounding the Battle of Hastings in 1066. In the feast scene a server wearing a napkin around his neck kneels before the high table where William the Conqueror, his nobles, and Bishop

Odo are having dinner. The towel and kneeling are significant, says Rickert, because four hundred years later it was in the code of courtesy outlined by *John Russell's Book of Nurture* (ca. 1470). Russell, who learned courtesy on the job as an officer of royal households, writes instructions for the medieval reader, presumably young noblemen in training for service: "put a towel around your neck, for that is courtesy; and put one end of it mannerly over the left arm; and on the same place your lord's napkin.... Carry a towel about your neck when serving your lord, bow to him, uncover your bread and set it by the salt. Look that all have knives, spoons and napkins, and always when you pass your lord, see that you bow your knees.... be cheerful, courteous of knee, soft of speech" (Rickert 1908). Today the best-trained waiters still carry that white folded towel over the left arm, and they "bow" by lowering the head respectfully. The *chef de cuisine* in his white double-breasted coat wears a small white towel tied around his neck.

Even the earliest English poetry shows an awareness of manners and suggests a code of ritualized behavior. "Wealhtheow forth, queen of Hrothgar, heedful of courtesy," begins a passage from the Anglo-Saxon medieval epic poem *Beowulf* (ca. A.D. 700). Queen Wealhtheow, the ideal gentlewoman and the perfect hostess, moves seamlessly through the hall offering food and drink to guests.

A quick reality check is in order, lest we overly romanticize ceremonious medieval feasting. Conditions included both splendor and squalid sanitation, and there was always the potential for violence to erupt over a disagreement in the dining hall. Yes, royal clothing was elaborate, often embroidered in gold and decorated with jewels like the gold chalices used by royals at the table. But palaces and castles were cold, and the floors were often littered with animal excrement, garbage, even human waste. As late as the fifteenth century, English kings took weekly (at best!) "bird baths," as my mother called the sponging of head, legs, and other strategic areas, and when they had a proper bath it was a big event—a reason to celebrate, and you can imagine why. But the lower classes, servants in upper-class households, may have bathed once a year, if that. The stench must have been overwhelming. Teaching and achieving high standards of behavior was no small task. The oldest existing treatises on manners from the early thirteenth century emphasize cleanliness (and you can see why!), physical restraint (minimizing bodily movements that are not only ungraceful but threatening to other diners), and respectful speech that communicates consideration of others—themes repeated in this discussion and the foundations of all eating rules today.

In the prologue of the fourteenth-century poem *Canterbury Tales*, Chaucer makes fun of the Prioress because her fastidious table manners, like her fluent French learned without even setting foot in France, smacked of affected gentility. When you read the following passage, keep in mind that in the Middle Ages diners are eating with their hands from communal bowls and drinking from one shared cup. Just as the Bible speaks of "bread" when referring to food, in this context "meat" (line 1) means "dinner."

> At meat her manners were well taught withal;
> No morsel from her lips did she let fall,
> Nor dipped her fingers in the sauce too deep;
> But she could carry a morsel up and keep
> The smallest drop from falling on her breast.
> For courtliness she had a special zest.
> And she would wipe her upper lip so clean
> That not a trace of grease was to be seen
> Upon the cup when she had drunk; to eat
> She reached a hand sedately for the meat.
> She certainly was very entertaining,
> Pleasant and in her ways, and straining,
> To counterfeit a courtly kind of grace
> A stately bearing fitting to her place.
> —Chaucer, *The Canterbury Tales*, Prologue

Medieval manners books were plentiful, but the first to be published was a fourteenth-century poem, *The Boke of Curtesye* (ca. 1350), both printed and translated into more modern English by William Caxton a century later in England (ca. 1477). Written in verse, *The Book of Courtesy* details an elaborate dining etiquette. Table setting was a ritual, as were the serving and consumption of dinner, especially for feasting. The senior ewerer in charge of hand washing and linens arranged the washing basins and all the napery (tablecloths, napkins, and towels). He supervised the laying of linens on the "board," often set on a dais for elevation and thus called "the high table," where the lord of the manor sat with his lady, knight, and squire. Two large, overlapping cloths were placed in the center of the table and a third, the *surnappe*, a large towel, went down the middle to protect the linens beneath during hand washing before and after the meal. The folding of the upper cloth, the direction of the folds and selvage, were specified and part of the ceremony. The *panter*, the household officer in charge of bread and the manor's pantry, laid the tables. He arranged the lord's *manchet* (bread roll), wrapped in a linen napkin, his knife, spoon, salt cellar, and *bread-trenchers* (square-cut slices of stale bread used as plates for meat). The knife, salt cellar, and goblet were on the right, the napkin and bread on the left, similar to the modern place setting minus the fork. Once complete, the place setting was covered with yet another towel.

When guests were seated and the place settings uncovered, the carver, "small towel upon his neck shall be seen," approached the lord, bowed and knelt, and ceremoniously unwrapped his bread, recalling John Russell's instructions. Next he cut a small plug from the ends of both manchet and trencher, and the panter tasted them along with the salt as a protection against poison. The ewerer strained water through a towel to clean it, covered the basin with the over-basin and yet another towel. He removed the covers to taste the water for poison before the carver poured the lord's cup. Again, the carver tasted the water before offering a cup to the knight and other important guests. The cupbearer knelt before the lord with his cup of wine, removed its cover, and he poured a few drops into the cover to taste yet again for poison. In the kitchen after the cook assayed the meat (checking for poison, of course), the server immediately covered it before taking it into the hall.

> The cook assays the meat undight,
> The sewer [server], he takes and covers aright.
> Whosoever takes that meat to bear,
> Shall not be so hardy the coverture to rear,
> For cold or hot, I warn you all,
> For suspicion of treason, as may befall.
> —*The Boke of Curtesye*, ca. 1350

After the long process, the marshal of the hall and cup-bearer tasted the lord's hand-washing water. The marshal even kissed the linen hand towel to detect poison, and then placed it on the lord's left shoulder, not in his lap as we do today. (Whew! We haven't even gotten to the lower tables!) Keeping one's hands above board was not only courtesy but a safety precaution: any activity in the lap suggested something unseemly like scratching, or it signaled imminent danger, such as reaching for a dagger. Today in many countries, and especially in Europe, it is still impolite if not taboo to hide one's hands below the table.

Many early manners books were written for children in rhyming verse that made rules easier to remember. *The ABC of Aristotle* offers charming instruction through playful verse, as do the rhyming verses of *Urbanitatis*, *Seager's School of Virtue*, and *Young Scholar's Paradise*. *How the Good Wife Taught her Daughter* (early to middle fourteenth century) is one of the few "conduct poems" written for lower-class women. Honor—namely virginal and wedded chastity—and thrift are central themes, the latter a bourgeois concern mentioned rarely in poems for the aristocracy. The good wife instructs the daughter to sell her homespun goods in the market and use the proceeds to pay her debts at the tavern. She warns against drunkenness, and she teaches street smarts, household management, and courteous behavior. How to attract and keep a husband (any man is better than no man!) and how to be a good housewife are among the goals.

> If any man offer thee courtship, and would marry thee,
> Look that thou scorn him not, whoever he be;
> But show it to thy friends and conceal it naught.
> —How the Good Wife Taught her Daughter [in Rickert 1908]

The most famous of medieval manners books is the fifteenth-century English *The Babees' Book*, translated from an anonymous Latin poem (see Rickert 1908). The book instructs manners and duties to young upper-class children, some of royal blood (not babies in the contemporary sense of the word). Although a handful of readers were princes and little lords and ladies in training, the real audience was children left without financial support by the system of primogeniture or by a father's reversal of fortune. These working children of aristocratic gentlemen were barred from the trades, and unless they were interested in the church or perhaps the law, the last resort was service in the household of a rich man of high rank. Going into "service" in fifteenth-century England, Rickert reminds us, did not have the same connotation it does today. Masters of important households took well-born youths under their wings and mentored them. The *bele babees* (literally, children of the court) performed menial tasks in exchange for an education—training in a skill and, most importantly, in manners, especially table manners—which could lead them out of service to a good marriage or socially acceptable work on the continent or back at court.

Similar to other medieval and early Renaissance children's books on manners, *The Babees' Book* speaks of courtesy and virtue in the same breath. They were synonymous. Cleanliness, noiselessness, and bodily control demonstrate self-respect and consideration of others, still the foundation of all eating rules. "Do not cut your meat like fieldmen who have such an appetite that they wreck not in that wise, where or when or how ungodly they hack at their meat; but sweet children, have always your delight in courtesy and in gentleness, and eschew boisterousness with all your might." *The Babees' Book* offers the same instruction we give children today: don't pick your nose, teeth, or nails at the table; don't blow your nose on the napkin; don't stuff your mouth with food and take a gulp of drink; eat quietly and without hanging your head over your plate; don't talk with a full mouth; don't burp in another's face; don't blow on hot food; and don't put your knife to your mouth!

Renaissance to Revolution

The Book of the Courtier (1528) by Count Baldesar Castiglione (1478–1529) and *Il Galateo, or About Manners* (1558) by the patrician Giovanni Della Casa (1503–1556) are among the most famous of all courtesy books. Although a generation apart, the two authors had much in common. Both were classically educated; they worked for kings, princes, and popes and traveled in the highest social circles; and they wrote in the context of the Italian Renaissance and the relentless wars of that time. Foreign invasions and power plays among Italian city-states were devastating economies and causing the reorganization of social and political institutions. This chaotic period of Italian history was also intellectually and artistically fertile. Della Casa and Castiglione shared the stage with stars like Machiavelli, Palladio, Leonardo da Vinci, Michelangelo, and Raphael, to name a few.

Whereas medieval books were often written in verse to help children remember their manners, *The Courtier* by Castiglione is written in dialogue for an educated, adult audience—the nobility who, by the way, already knew what to do at dinner. Castiglione's tone is philosophical rather than prescriptive, and though he may not explicitly discuss table manners he influenced generations of courtesy writers.

Castiglione began writing *The Courtier* "as a portrait of the Court of Urbino" and a tribute to the friends he had admired while in courtly service there. Almost twenty years after its inception, the final version of *The Courtier* completed in 1527 was a luminous depiction of court life in the Italian Renaissance and an unvarnished portrait of the perfect courtier, the noble gentleman, in his context. The book articulates the dilemma of an aristocratic ruling class responding to the pressures of political and social change that reduced them to "servants" of potentially corrupt or ignorant princes; it creates a new model of comportment that reconciles compromise—the loss of personal freedom and aggression—and the preservation of moral freedom (the true self). This new model has been called "the art of prince-pleasing." I might call it grace under pressure. Beyond prince-pleasing, the book's theme—that the image the courtier presents to himself, his prince, and the court (through education, dress, and manners) is crucial—anticipates social mobility.

The Courtier reads like the transcript of conversations taking place over four consecutive evenings in 1507 at the court of the Duke of Urbino where, in the music- and dance-filled salon, the main characters play a lively after-dinner parlor game that thinly veils serious discussion. (Each evening the game's topic is discussed and becomes a "book" or chapter.) To give weight and credibility to this rhetorical work, Castiglione uses the real names of people he admired and emulated for the main characters, because each in his or her own way possessed qualities, most of all honor and refined taste, that contributed to the ideal courtier. The speakers ask themselves what values and comportment, what skills, must the courtier possess to stay in the prince's favor and survive with dignity the unstable life at court. To answer this question, Castiglione reevaluates the autonomous feudal aristocrat—a skilled soldier often characterized as the chivalrous, rough-and-tumble knight in shining armor—and repackages him as the much tamed but still idealized Renaissance courtier: polite, educated, refined, self-controlled, well-spoken, and subordinate, yet still retaining knightly capabilities.

Whereas the medieval knight's lady love was an influential, essential part of her community, Castiglione's ideal Renaissance "Court Lady" is reduced to a decorative role: the gracious hostess who sets the tone at court. Her success depends on marrying well and shining as wife, mother, and mistress of her household. Granted the same education as men, with the exception of some "unbecoming" sporting activities, she is first and foremost physically beautiful; she is chaste, subordinate to her husband and the prince, and ultimately the representation of self-control and good manners—the "trophy wife," as we say today.

"Medieval courtesy, as set forth in the earliest etiquette books, romances, and rules of love [in the eleventh and twelfth centuries], shaped the man primarily to please the lady," says Joan Kelly-Gadol in her essay "Did Women Have a Renaissance?" "In the thirteenth and fourteenth centuries, rules for women, and strongly patriarchal ones at that, entered French and Italian etiquette books, but not until the Renaissance reformulation of courtly manners and romantic love is it evident how the ways of the lady came to be determined by men in the context of the early modern state." Castiglione, like other courtesy writers of the period, was no exception. He wrote his book for men.

Renaissance aspirational ideals were founded on a belief in self-cultivation through education, and they were realized through *imitatio*—the imitation of past models and abstracted standards of perfection. Like the cultural reformers who preceded him, Castiglione looked to the ancient Greeks and Romans for guidance and inspiration. His text includes abundant references to classical writers.

In the Dedication he writes, "There is the Idea of perfect Republic [Plato's *Republic*], the perfect King [Xenophon's *Cyropaedia*], and the perfect Orator [Cicero's *De oratore*], so likewise there is that of the perfect Courtier." His Renaissance courtier, like his chivalric predecessor, was fierce and brave, but now must be educated in Latin and Greek; he must study the classics and modern French, Spanish, and Italian. As the noble gentleman he must have a working knowledge of science, art, and literature, as well as the ability to draw, paint, write, sing, act, play a variety of instruments, and dance gracefully while maintaining athletic skills like jousting, vaulting, dueling, horsemanship, swimming, wrestling. He must be good-looking and affable, humorous, skilled at joke-telling, virtuous, sympathetic, wise, and if possible, of noble birth. (They must have had to remind themselves to breathe!) You see where the term Renaissance man/woman originates. In the preface of *The Courtier*, Javitch explains that "sixteenth-century readers were fully accustomed to being asked to exceed their capacities, to emulate models that were, by definition, unreachable." A model so idealistic, so lofty as Castiglione's courtier, only made it more deserving of imitation—and inspiring. "The book asks those who would emulate its model to stretch their virtuosity and their virtue." And if courtiers reading the book find this perfection unattainable, writes Castiglione in the Dedication of *The Courtier*, "the one who comes nearest to it will be the most perfect; as when many archers shoot at a target and none of them hits the bull's eye, the one who comes closest is surely better than all the rest."

Mediocrità, the moderation of extremes, must be expressed at all times and with discipline. Dress well, clothes neither too plain nor too fancy. Everything must express *grazia*, gracefulness, whether God-given, stolen, or selectively imitated. "Our Courtier must steal this grace from those who seem to him to have it, taking from each the part that seems worthy of praise," writes Castiglione. The acquisition of grace and the exercise of moderation are closely aligned with *sprezzatura*, the most famous concept of *The Courtier*: "But, having thought many times already about how this grace is acquired (leaving aside those who have it from the stars), I have found quite a universal rule…and that is to avoid affectation in every way possible as though it were some very rough and dangerous reef; and (to pronounce a new word perhaps) to practice in all things a certain *sprezzatura* [nonchalance], so as to conceal art and make whatever is done or said appear to be without effort and almost without any thought about it. And I believe much grace comes of this." D'Epiro and Pinkowish liken *sprezzatura* to a "social mask" that disguises the separation between appearance and reality. It is, they say, "the very patina of civilization." They also remind us that "this still-important Italian obsession—*far una bella figura* (to make a good impression, cut a fine figure) is at the heart of Castiglione's vision of life as social artifice." Berger writes that in this unstable era, the threat of disempowerment was real, and the effortlessness of *sprezzatura* was manliness "worn like a velvet glove that exhibits the contours of the handiness it conceals. But of course the glove could be filled with wet clay." Berger wonders if "this signifier of virile manhood" disguises weakness or anxiety. Deconstructionists have differing opinions about *sprezzatura*, both cynical and sympathetic. This is not surprising since today, in some circles, courtliness is viewed with suspicion as snobbery—hypocritical and "too good to be true"—while others regard the behavior as genuinely thoughtful and respectful. In my opinion, the "social mask" is not intended to conceal the wearer's *true* nature, nor is it necessarily deceitful. The mask is the filter, the human mechanism for impulse control that is the hallmark of civilized behavior. Well-practiced, effortless grace and self-control are integral to an individual's character.

To bring this concept of nonchalance/*sprezzatura* to the table (and down to earth), imagine arriving at a dinner party only to find the hostess half-dressed and in hair rollers, frantically setting the table and washing dishes. (Alas, this was yours truly hosting her own birthday party a few years ago.) Guests are set on edge, to say the least. I'll invoke the dressing metaphor here: the naked truth about all the work that goes into a party, or really anything you do for another person, is that undressed work makes guests uneasy. A beautiful dinner party is, in a sense, a work of art, and *sprezzatura* makes it a gift.

The Courtier was published by the Aldine Press in Venice in 1528 and was almost immediately translated into Spanish, French, Latin, German, Polish, and English. It was lauded as a masterpiece of literature, a work of art because of the picture of the perfect courtier and lady of court it paints. Although not written as a guide to manners, it soon functioned as one, setting the modern standard for honorable gentlemanly behavior. That it elevated the art of prince-pleasing to such a "noble level" explains its continuous appeal, according to Javitch: "The uplifting effects of the book could only increase later in the sixteenth century, as courts became more despotic or monarchs, at least, became increasingly dominant and restricted their courtiers' freedom of expression and of action even further." For four hundred years after the initial publication of *The Courtier*, the courtesy it encouraged remained the standard throughout Europe, surviving the French Revolution and persisting into the twentieth century when the First World War leveled society. And it lives on in small pockets of American culture today. Indirection, tact, deference, nonchalance are not only revered but tightly woven into the fabric of the genteel southern American model. I hate to disappoint, but this model is one that I cannot always practice perfectly!

Il Galateo, or About Manners, by Italian poet, translator, and cleric Monsignor Giovanni Della Casa, was written in Venice between 1552 and 1555. Della Casa was profoundly influenced by the brutality and political chaos that continued into the second quarter of the sixteenth century. Undoubtedly, he was also influenced by the monumental

The Courtier, but his treatise on manners takes a very different approach. Writing thirty years after Castiglione, Della Casa counsels the ruling class and a now growing middle class. He never speaks of kings and princes or ladies of the court. He never mentions women at all. There are no idealized concepts, although Christian values lie just below the surface. Instead, he "dresses" as a fictional character *idiota*, the illiterate old uncle who speaks in homey colloquialisms to give down-to-earth advice gained from real-life situations. The uncle's style is modest and a little ragged: If you see something disgusting on the road, don't call it to your companion's attention, or worse, say, "Now sir, please smell how this stinks." (My mother would never let me say "stinks.") He asks his nephew, "Now what do we think the bishop and his noble friends would have said to those we sometimes see, who totally oblivious like pigs with their snouts in the swill, never raise their faces nor their eyes, let alone their hands, from the food in front of them? Or those who eat or rather gulp down their food with both their cheeks puffed out as if they were blowing a trumpet or blowing on a fire? Or those who soil their hands nearly up to the elbows, and dirty their napkins worse than their toilet towels?" (Della Casa 1986).

The first time I read *Galateo*, I was sitting alone at a secluded table in the tomb-silent stacks of the UNC graduate library. Reading quietly and in earnest, I was soon laughing out loud! "And when you blow your nose you should not open your handkerchief and look inside, as if pearls or rubies might have descended from your brain." Speaking of noses, the narrator, Old Uncle, cautions that at the dinner table, don't put your nose over someone else's glass of wine or food or let someone else put theirs over yours. Something disgusting may drop from his nose, and he doesn't mean diamonds and pearls! Della Casa's *idiota* displays no indirection and bluntly gets right to the point: good manners make people want to love you, want to live with you. Uncouth manners make people hate you. There is no law against these crimes, but nature has a way of punishing them: no one will want to be around you. "And just as great sins harm us greatly, these light faults are a nuisance and bother us often. Men fear wild beasts but have no fear of smaller animals such as mosquitoes or flies; still, because these insects are constant pests, men complain more often about them than about wild beasts" (Della Casa 1986). In other words, irritating people are disliked as much as or more than evil ones. Della Casa's tone is practical, his advice experiential and prescriptive. If we are going to live together in close proximity, not alone or in the desert, manners are easy to practice and useful, and "rich and powerful precisely because they involve nothing but words and gestures."

Although some things are so offensive to the senses and the intellect they must be avoided altogether—and Della Casa describes them with gusto like an adolescent boy—what is appropriate comportment, dress, speech, or table manners depends on the circumstances. He advocates a kind of relativism: let customs guide. Bucking the system is contradiction and therefore unmannerly and ill-advised, as offensive as mocking, slander, gossip, and long-windedness.

Just like Castiglione, Della Casa speaks of grace and moderation, decorum and virtue, but as applied to daily life in the context of making a good impression. This is not about vanity or hollow ceremonies. D'Epiro and Pinkowish remind us that "Castiglione's keyword is *sprezzatura*, and Della Casa stresses *leggiadria*, an elegant grace that emanates like an aura from one's actions, words, sentiments, gestures deriving from the Renaissance virtues of harmony, concordance, reasonableness and proportion." Don't overdo frilly clothes, fancy manners, bowing and scraping, and flaunting flourishes as the Spanish did when they occupied Italy in the Early Modern period. Don't walk in the street too slowly or too quickly. Keep up with the traffic, and dress appropriately.

Considering the violence and political turmoil of the first half of the sixteenth century and the author's professional disappointments and personal losses, translators Eisenbichler and Bartlett suggest that Della Casa's motivation for *Galateo* was restorative: "Order, precedence, manners and rules provide structure to both societies and to an individual's life....the lessons of *Galateo* could offer comfort and useful advice, allowing each man the opportunity to improve his own immediate world, to cultivate his own garden."

Galateo was published posthumously in Venice in 1558 and has never gone out of print. In Italy *Galateo* is still synonymous with manners. "He doesn't know his *Galateo*!" is a way of saying a person is rude, *maleducato*. The specificity and practicality of *Galateo* made it groundbreaking, laying the foundation for modern manners books.

The famous *La Bienséance* [*manners*] *de la conversation entre les hommes* (*Decency of conversation among men*), first published anonymously and in French in 1595, is an etiquette book conspicuously based on *Galateo*. (This next part may seem like a whodunit/detective story, so stay with me.) It was actually the work of "residents," perhaps scholars at the Jesuit College of La Fleche in western France, who subsequently sent the work to the abbey at Pont-à-Mousson in northeast France. There, Father Perin translated the book into Latin and added a table-manners section of his own devising. His book was complete by 1617. The book of maxims in Latin made its way to Paris in 1638, where it was well received and translated into Spanish, German, and back into French by 1640. In about the same year, *La Bienséance de la conversation entre les hommes* was translated from French into English as *Youth's Behaviour, or Decency in conversation amongst men* by Francis Hawkins (1628–1681). We know that the fourth edition of *Youth's Behaviour* was printed in 1646 in London by W. Wilson for William Lee. For the next several decades there were eleven editions to which English writers added rules.

The saga continues a century later in the American South. John Washington, the great-grandfather of the first president of the United States, migrated from England to Virginia in the mid-seventeenth century. George Washington, the son of gentleman farmer and tobacco planter Augustine Washington and his second wife Mary Ball Washington, was born in 1732 and raised in Westmoreland County, Virginia. His father and half-brothers were educated in England, and were it not for the death of his father when he was only eleven, George, too, might have returned to England for secondary schooling.

In the 1740s, before the age of sixteen, young George learned penmanship and proper behavior by copying into a school notebook 110 maxims from the *Rules of Civility and Decent Behavior*, clearly based on the rules of etiquette spelled out in the much older books *Bienséance* and *Youth's Behaviour*, and of course *Galateo*. It is not known for sure how a copy of *Rules* got into George Washington's hands. That his father or half-brothers brought it from England is a good guess. Over and over, he wrote out the rules until they were not only memorized but internalized. As an adult Washington was a living example of the principles behind the maxims: honor, deference, courtesy. He was known and admired for his impeccable manners and self-control (he used the maxims to control his famously sharp temper), his humility, his respect for and consideration of others—qualities that molded both his personal life and his leadership style. After he served as the first commander-in-chief of the Continental Army with victorious results, at the end of the Revolutionary War his adoring officers wished to make him king of America. Vice President John Adams argued that Washington should be addressed as "His Majesty, the President" or simply "His Highness." Who better to lead a new nation than a man who wore the clothes of a general and the manners of a prince?

Born in Holland the same year as George Washington, Philip Stanhope was the illegitimate son of the erudite statesman, diplomat, and wit Philip Dormer Stanhope, Fourth Earl of Chesterfield (1694–1773), author of *Lord*

Chesterfield's Letters to His Son: On the Art of Becoming a Man of the World and a Gentleman. While Washington was acquiring the knowledge, morals, and manners of an eighteenth-century Virginia gentleman, an education lovingly overseen by his older half-brother and surrogate father Lawrence Washington, Stanhope's overbearing lord-father orchestrated his education from afar. Tutors supervised Stanhope's classical curriculum and accompanied him on the Grand Tour to acquire politesse and political savvy. Four hundred letters from Lord Chesterfield to his son and godson—letters the author never dreamed would be revealed to the public—document his relentless teaching and preaching. "The end which I propose by your education," the lord writes his son, "and which (if you please) I shall certainly attain, is to unite in you all the knowledge of a scholar with the manners of a courtier; and to join, what is seldom joined in any of my countrymen, books and the world."

Mentioned repeatedly in his letters is the advice to wear the mask of geniality that clothes Machiavellian intent. "The height of abilities is, to have *volto sciolto*, and *pensieri stretti*; that is, a frank, open, and ingenuous exterior, with a prudent and reserved interior; to be upon your own guard, and yet, by a seeming natural openness, to put people off of theirs. Depend upon it, nine in ten of every company you are in, will avail themselves of every indiscreet and unguarded expression of yours, if they can turn it to their own advantage. A prudent reserve is therefore as necessary, as a seeming openness is prudent."

Letters owed much of its success to *The Courtier*, although Chesterfield mentions neither Castiglione nor Machiavelli, to whom he is often compared. Like Castiglione, Chesterfield was a courtier for a brief period. Mirroring the requirements for the idealized Renaissance courtier, he urges his son to master foreign languages; read the Greek and Roman classics, as well as contemporary literature; learn about art, history, and economics; gain proficiency in athletics and social dancing; and above all, acquire grace. "The Graces, the Graces; remember the Graces!" he ends a letter in 1749. However, his grace is not like Della Casa's *leggiadria*, a grace that emanates from the soul, nor Castiglione's graceful *sprezzatura*, nonchalance to conceal effort. Chesterfield's stylized manners are calculated, political, and practiced for an end: "There is a certain dignity of manners absolutely necessary, to make even the most valuable character either respected or respectable." The well-mannered project credibility and command respect. Chesterfield's ideology is success.

Letitia Baldridge, in her *New Complete Guide to Executive Manners*, explains that today manners contribute to, and detract from, successful careers—especially table manners: "No aspect of an executive's *persona* is as highly visible and capable of directing a sometimes cruel spotlight on him as the quality of his table manners." Executives, however, are not the only ones vulnerable to criticism. Consider that 75 percent of all business is transacted around food. Lunch, dinner, and even breakfast are the setting for recruiting, interviews, and annual meetings, and the table is the place where deals are made, jobs won and lost. It is also the place where table manners are scrutinized. In today's highly competitive business environment with equally qualified professionals vying for a shrinking number of positions, employers look for reasons to eliminate applicants and even seasoned employees; many will turn the dining room into their test site. I know a young woman who was not promoted to a job in university development because she drank coffee with the spoon in the cup. This small misstep screamed, "No social skills!"

Describing the less than ideal fellow (hypothetically seeking employment), Chesterfield writes the following:

> At dinner his awkwardness distinguishes itself
> particularly, as he has more to do: there he holds his
> knife, fork, and spoon differently from other people;
> eats with his knife to the great danger of his mouth;
> picks his teeth with his fork, and puts his spoon, which

has been in his throat twenty times, into the dishes again. If he is to carve, he can never hit the joint, but, in his vain efforts to cut through the bone, scatters the sauce in everybody's face. He generally daubs himself with soup and grease, though his napkin is commonly stuck through a buttonhole and tickles his chin. When he drinks he infallibly coughs in his glass, and besprinkles the company. Besides all this, he has strange tricks and gestures; such as snuffing up his nose, making faces, putting his fingers in his nose, or blowing it and looking afterwards in his handkerchief, so as to make the company sick. His hands are troublesome to him when he has not something in them, and he does not know where to put them; but they are in perpetual motion between his bosom and his breeches: he does not wear his clothes [dress well], and, in short, does nothing, like other people. All this I own is not in any degree criminal; but it is highly disagreeable and ridiculous in company, and ought most carefully to be avoided, by whoever desires to please. (Chesterfield 2008)

Behaving badly is not discouraged on moral grounds or because it breaks rules of polite society, but because it endangers one's success. "Remember that to please is to prevail, or at least a necessary step to it."

Although a staunch Francophile and fluent in French, Lord Chesterfield writes to Stanhope, who is traveling in Italy, that he should learn the *garbo* (politeness), the *leggiadria*, the *gentilezza* (kindness) of the Italians. The best place to learn the Graces he believes is Italy, specifically Turin. "I have known as many well-bred, pretty men come from Turin as from any part of Europe. The late King Victor Amédée took great pains to form such of his subjects as were of any consideration both to business and manners." He writes that in Turin, Stanhope will find good models for his own self-cultivation, a reference to the Renaissance concept of *imitatio*. "Observe every word, look, motion of those who are allowed to be the most accomplished persons there. Observe their natural and careless, but genteel air; their unembarrassed good breeding; their unassuming, but yet unprostituted dignity."

By the mid-seventeenth century, Italian style was eclipsed by high society in Paris and the court of Versailles, the new pinnacle of fashion and elegant behavior. Unlike the *mediocrità* of Italian manners, French etiquette was extreme. Manners were political for the autocratic Louis XIV. Praised for creating absolute monarchical rule that lasted 72 years and stabilized France, and for successfully taking on the mercantile system, which increased trade through exportation of luxury goods, he used excessive etiquette as a control tactic. Its stiffness and artifice were reflected in the stiffness and artifice of court dress and the restrictive behavior required.

The word *etiquette* came into use during Louis XIV's reign. *Etiquette*, originally *étiquet*, and Old French *estiquet*, meant *ticket*, *label*, or *card*, according to the *Shorter O.E.D*. Courtiers and guests were reminded of the rigid and complex rules of Louis XIV's court etiquette with strategically displayed cards bearing lists of the do's and don'ts of dining and comportment. He commanded nobility to live at Versailles in what was tantamount to a state of royal house arrest. They could not walk in the gardens or move through the palace without "tickets" posted everywhere. With his self-serving etiquette, Louis XIV dominated manners in all things—not just rules of his dinner table. He manipulated thought and controlled conversation and dress, overemphasizing the importance of lavish clothes and jewels and nearly sending courtiers into bankruptcy. Some say he wanted to keep them powerless, and debt does just that. His goal was also to show off to the world his power and superiority.

Sun King and paragon of style, Louis XIV was a short man who wore high heels. He painted his heels red as a sign of power and nobility—one who neither toiled nor trod on common soil. Only approved members of court were allowed to paint their heels red as well. If these individuals went out of favor and wore the red heel, forgetting to remove it or deliberately wearing it as a status symbol, they were beheaded. This is an example of sumptuary law that for centuries regulated dress and consumption as a way to maintain social hierarchy. In Louis's court there was dressing for success, as well as survival.

French etiquette of the late eighteenth century during the reign of Louis XVI was even more rigid and unnatural. Red heels remained the royal style: *"Talons rouges* [red heels] became a synonym for French courtiers' futile insolence,"* writes Mansel. The French Revolution brutally ended the monarchy and the reign of the mightily mannered, turning everything upside down. Before the revolution, aristocratic clothing and manners displayed wealth and rank. After the French Revolution and during the Reign of Terror, the rich were guillotined. Literally dressing for survival, noblemen tossed out their frilly, ribbon-laced silk knee pants and powdered wigs to don the long, loose trousers of the working class. Intellectuals wore a *himation* à la Socrates. Aristocratic ladies wouldn't be caught dead in corseted silk gowns, jewels, and towering, confectionary hairstyles that were held together with flour and water (the eighteenth-century version of hair spray), styles so voluminous that cartoonists depicted the dos as tiered wedding cakes or sailing ships sitting on their heads. After the revolution, the same ladies wore classic Grecian hairstyles or, for a moment, a macabre style: short haircuts or simple updos that bared the neck and a red throat ribbon instead of jewels, referring to the haircut of guillotined victims. Austere, classically inspired gowns made of simple muslin and worn with little or no undergarment replaced the corseted, pre-revolutionary frou-frou. Still slaves to fashion, some women wet the muslin chemises to make them cling to the body, imitating the body-revealing styles seen in ancient Greek sculpture. Cases of pneumonia during winter months dampened the zeal of these foolish fashionistas.

Like clothing styles, manners in the period were political and adapting to a radically new caste system. The French Revolution sent shock waves throughout Europe, much as the political and social upheavals and counter-culture of the 1960s in the United States disrupted norms beyond its borders. In reaction to the French Revolution's "corruption of continental manners," explains Pine-Coffin in a modern translation of *Il Galateo* (Pine-Coffin 1958), English manners stiffened.

American Refinement

Emerging from its provincial and rural past, mid-eighteenth-century America was transformed by theories of classical republicanism and neoclassical aesthetics, a transatlantic phenomenon that affected revolutionary political thought, education, literature, art and architecture, and clothing styles. Only a decade before its own revolutionary movement (1787–1799), France participated in the American Revolution. The Marquis de Lafayette (1757–1834), commissioned Major General by Congress, fought alongside General Washington. Benjamin Franklin (1706–1790) and Thomas Jefferson (1743–1826) served as trade ministers to France and immersed themselves in Parisian social and cultural life. In spite of the Revolution, America maintained close cultural and commercial ties with Britain. John Adams (1735–1826) was the first American ambassador to Britain, a signatory of the Treaty of Paris, and a negotiator of trade relations between the United States and Prussia and commercial agreements with Portugal and the Netherlands. Few if any early American leaders had polish equal to that of European royal company. As they formed a new and independent government, our founding fathers were torn between deliberate simplicity that conformed to the new democratic republican ideals and aristocratic gentility. Motivated by social anxiety or reverse snobbery, each sought a deportment style suited to various audiences.

Some even resorted to theatricality: Franklin wore a coonskin cap in Paris!

George Washington was "to the manor born," raised at the Belvoir mansion and Mt. Vernon. His education included training in the formal, pre-Revolutionary Virginia genteel manners that defined the upper classes. For the Tidewater elite—planters and merchants living along the Potomac and James Rivers and North Carolina Tidewater—the English country gentleman was the model of propriety, the embodiment of sophisticated behaviors that evolved from those of Italian courtiers and French royalty centuries earlier. Gentility in all its manifestations supported class authority and reinforced a defined social order. Their great houses, education, clothes, and manners suggested power and commanded respect.

Consider Westover Plantation, circa 1730, in Charles City County owned by William Byrd II (1674–1744), one of the richest men in all of the colonies and the founder of Richmond, Virginia; Berkeley Plantation in Fredericksburg, completed in 1726, home to Benjamin Harrison V, a signer of the Declaration of Independence; and Stratford Hall Plantation in Westmoreland County, 1738, boyhood home of the brothers Richard Henry Lee and Francis Lightfoot Lee, also signers of the Declaration of Independence. At Stratford Hall in the great house, as the family's sumptuous residence is called, there is a French crystal chandelier in the great hall, fine portraits in the drawing room, and in the elegant dining room a table and chairs, china, crystal, and silver cutlery including knives, forks, and spoons for table settings, a rarity in the early Colonial period.

The libraries of these and many other Tidewater mansions contained English translations of books like Baldesar Castiglione's *The Book of the Courtier*; Giovanni Della Casa's *Il Galateo*; Richard Brathwaite's *The English Gentleman*; and, according to Wilson, the most influential of all for the southern elite, *The Whole Duty of Man*, one of the first books printed in Virginia and the popular source for guidelines on behavior until the mid-nineteenth century and not just for southerners. In a letter to his wife, Benjamin Franklin urged his daughter to read and re-read *The Whole Duty of Man*. An English Protestant ecclesiastical work written anonymously and published with an introduction by Henry Hammond in 1658, it derives from Christian tradition (Anglican) and not classical *urbanitas* or Renaissance courtliness. In England, the original audience for the book was made up of small business owners, families on farms, presumably all modest folk who were encouraged to look inward for the graces—love, beauty, accomplishment—and to denounce ostentation. Dress was for modesty, comfort, and survival but not to impress.

One of the earliest American courtesy manuals, *The School of Good Manners*, was written by a Boston schoolmaster, Eleazar Moody, in 1715, suggesting that there was an awareness of fashionable gentility in Puritan New England. The volume is split into two sections: the first part instructs children in the principles of a proper Puritan education, purity of thought being one of the main tenets; and the second part, "borrowed" from a British manners book printed in 1565 in London, is an etiquette "book" with rules for cleanliness, comportment, and table manners, although tables for dining and even chairs for sitting while eating were not an essential component of the earliest colonial households. Still, eating like a caveman was frowned upon, and Moody establishes rules. *The School of Good Manners*, a manners manual, and *The Whole Duty of Man*, a guidebook of morality, were often bound together in one volume. Similarly, the eighteenth-century gentry blended apparently unrelated ideals into a single code of behavior. Manners equaled morals.

The refinement of America really began around 1690, says Bushman. The concept of "refinement" is based on a classical aspirational ideal revitalized by the Italian Renaissance, an ideal encompassing belief in the transformative effects of education, self-cultivation, and the acquisition of grace. Bushman cites words like "genteel," "civil," "urbane," words first used to describe courtiers. Gentility liberated imagination, a "powerful impulse" to beautify houses, landscapes, towns, behavior: "every scene was to be turned into a picture." The dark side of this campaign, says Bushman, was that the ugly had to be identified first to make it beautiful, and promoters of beauty criticized everything. Self-cultivation, then, required vigilant self-awareness and self-criticism.

At the time of the American Revolution gentility was extending further and further into the middle class, but as Bushman clarifies, "gentility flecked lives without coloring them." Average households might contain one book and only a few pieces of silver cutlery; they might also have a simple garden. Then parlors were added to some houses; farm hands became skilled craftsmen making refined tables, chairs, highboys, and what-nots to furnish parlors. A 1790s phenomenon, the oval dinner table was designed to make formal dining egalitarian by eliminating the hierarchical head of the table. Slowly but surely sets of chairs made their way into middle-class dining rooms. Machines increased the production of goods that supplied the middle classses with what Bushman calls "vernacular gentility," the trappings of the landed gentry associated with "the good life" of ease and leisure, but most importantly, with respectability. American pioneers in manufacturing devised ways to reproduce in cotton the look of fancy European silk damask and imported chintz used for tablecloths, upholstery, and clothing. At the turn of the nineteenth century there were a few ready-to-wear shops that sold affordable clothes, albeit of a lower quality and less detailed than the custom-made equivalent worn by the gentry. Brooks Brothers opened its doors in 1818. Meanwhile, the upper classes feverishly pursued luxury.

Post-Revolutionary clothing styles for men changed the most, beginning with long pants taking the place of knee britches made of silks and satins in bright colors and patterns. By mid-nineteenth century the matched suit comprised of coat, vest, and trousers was called the "ditto" suit. By the end of the century it was made of drab colors to blend in with the dirt and soot of industrial cities, a uniform for businessmen that made one man look like the next for a double-ditto effect.

Greek-inspired clothing reflecting classical republican simplicity was the style for American women in the first decade of the nineteenth century. A variant of the French post-Revolutionary muslin chemise, the empire dress was a tall slender column of white cotton faille, fine muslin imported from India, or gossamer silk, high-waisted with a small capped sleeve referring to that of an Ionic *chiton*. Large paisley shawls from India draped about the shoulders took the place of the *himation*; stoles smaller in size were the accessory for spring and summer. For evening, lace or something close to our modern tulle was sometimes draped over the head mimicking styles depicted in Greek and Roman artifacts. Diadems anchored soft Grecian hairdos; shoes had flat heels for comfort and mobility. Ironically, many women continued to wear corsets under these loose-fitting unpretentious dresses. By 1820 only vestiges of classical influence on clothing styles remained. Skirts widened as did the breadth of the neckline emphasizing the upper body; hemlines raised to ankle or "tea length" were decorated with fussy trims and ruffles as were the fuller sleeves; emphasis on the waistline was back in style and the corset was again required equipment to support the hourglass silhouette. When the bustle reappeared in the late 1820s the neoclassical aesthetic in clothing styles was gone for good, and increasingly lavish styles veered dangerously close to French pre-Revolutionary extravagances.

Godey's Lady's Book, published by Louis A. Godey in Philadelphia from 1830 to 1878, showcased complicated new styles. Comparable in many ways to the twenty-first-century *Vogue* that offers articles on a variety of topics unrelated to clothing, *Godey's Magazine and Lady's Book*, as it was sometimes referred to, featured original poems, articles about gardening; manners and education; sheet music (for example, a mazurka composed for the piano-forte for *Godey's*); engravings; and explanations of clothing styles including a pattern or two for the home sewers. (Elias Howe patented the first American sewing machine in 1846.) A hand-tinted fashion plate was the frontispiece for each issue. The July 1859 fashion plate displays dress styles for young girls and adolescents: flounced skirts, ruffles, and fancy petticoats bordered with lace ruled the day. Sara Hale, editor-in-chief of *Godey's* and author of "Mary Had a Little Lamb," held up Queen Victoria as a role model. The young Victoria's intelligence and morals as well as her fashion sense—especially her choice of a white wedding dress—influenced American readers.

Beginning in the early Victorian era heavy padded undergarments, crinolines, bosom enhancers, and corsets restricted movement and heightened the artificiality of the costume and stiffened both the posture and behavior of the wearer. Around 1850 boned petticoats eliminated the need for multiple underskirts and crinolines to hold the skirt out. At first made of whale bones, by the 1860s the hoops were circles of watch-spring steel so light that it allowed skirts to become fuller and fuller until they were a fire hazard, not only because the materials were so flammable but because the wearer could not get through doorways to escape. How one walked and sat in gargantuan skirts became part of etiquette, especially critical in the dining room. To complicate matters, the rules of formal dining were gradually changing. Whereas the communal and intimate *service à la française* emboldened the host and guests to pick and choose from a multitude of platters set on the table at once, thus creating their own menus, *service à la russe* gave the chef and lady of the house total control of menu planning. Waiters brought out one course at a time, each requiring its own dishes, cutlery, and method of consumption. The diners were, in a sense, a captive audience. They were both performers and audience, watching and being watched. Etiquette books of the period included exquisitely detailed explanations of the corseted manners accompanying elaborate table setting as a refresher course for the initiated and as a primer for the growing middle-class readership. Like dancing around hoop skirts—an acquired skill for gentlemen as well as the ladies wearing them—the new table manners would take practice.

In the hoop-skirted South, communities were smaller, and there was accountability and a sense of personal responsibility to follow customs. Relatively speaking, the South was a matriarchal society in which women taught manners and morals to children, and smoothed the rough edges of men. However, as much as southerners stressed conformity to the prescribed code, they valued (and still value) individualism. Every town, every family had its cherished eccentric. In my father's family the eccentric, or one of them, was his cousin: a brilliant lawyer, professor of classics at the University of North Carolina, father of a Pulitzer–prize-winning newspaper editor. At dinner, when passed the communal bowl of spinach, he served himself *all* of the spinach if he were so inclined. Never mind his Tidewater Virginia ancestry. Legend has it that whenever asked to say grace before dinner he exclaimed, "For Christ's sake!" and lowering his head and voice, "For Christ's sake. Amen." That was it, every time. His fellow diners carried on ever so politely as if nothing rude or irreverent had happened. (Funny, isn't it, that table manners are used to summarize a personality? I know of otherwise accomplished people spoken of as "knife-lickers" or "stabbers," referring to their crude hold of knife and fork.) Yes, southerners have deep respect for manners, and this respect has been the counterbalance to individualism, says Wilson. "Southern manners were not only a community binding force, an agreed upon code for groups to aspire to; they were divisive, separating those with manners from those without." That may have been true, but stiff manners were never part of aristocratic southern culture. Remember that *sprezzatura*, making something difficult appear effortless, is second nature in the genteel South. A condescending attitude was not part of the culture, either, at least not in my experience. With ease and charm and above all humor—often self-deprecating humor—southerners display courtesy.

As Americans left their small towns, where everyone knew their names, and settled in cities, especially northern industrial cities, they moved at an accelerated tempo among strangers. Anonymity replaced accountability. People who did not know each other judged on appearance and comportment. But what happened to the classical republican ideals of democracy and simplicity? What happened to the Puritan and Anglican morality of manners? "Gentility was worldly not godly, it was hierarchical not egalitarian, and it favored leisure and consumption over work and thrift," Bushman writes. "These values ran at cross purposes with religion, republicanism, and the work ethic, powerful complexes of values subscribed by the same people who wanted to become genteel. But instead of leading to competition for dominance, as might be expected, in most instances the result of the interplay was mutual exchange and compromise." Bushman asserts that as allies capitalism and gentility molded the modern economy. "The refinement of America involved the capture of aristocratic culture for use in a republican society."

In this period of westward expansion and international trade, people and goods traveled back and forth most frequently across the Atlantic and the English Channel. In the cross-pollination of ideas and customs, European etiquette was still the model for Americans. *The Gentleman and Lady's Book of Politeness and Propriety of Deportment: dedicated to the youth of both sexes* by Elisabeth Celnart (1796–1865) was translated from the sixth Paris edition and published in 1833 in Boston. The preface, written by "The Translator," as he signs his name, explains that because the book was popular and well-respected in France, "the country we consider as the genial soil of politeness," the publishers offer this translation as a service to readers on this side of the Atlantic. "Some visitors in our country, whose own manners have not always given them a right to be censors of others, have very freely told us what we ought *not* to do; and it will be useful to know from respectable authority, what is done in polished society in Europe, and, of course, what we *ought to do*, in order to avoid all censure. This object, we are confident, will be more efficiently accomplished by the study of principles and rules contained in the present volume, than by any other of the kind." Qualifying the accolade, the translator continues: "We are aware, that a man can no more acquire the ease and elegance of a finished gentleman, by any manual of this kind, than in the fine arts he could become a skillful painter or sculptor by studying books alone, without practice. It is, however, equally true, that the principles of Politeness may be studied, as well as the principles of the arts. At the same time, intercourse with polite society, in other words, *practice*, as in the case of the arts, must do the rest."

In her introduction Madame Celnart writes, "Propriety of Deportment, or *bienséance*, is a happy union of the moral and the graceful." It is a result of self-knowledge, respect for the rights of others, and a realization that surrendering self-interests for the sake of good social interactions is "a sacred requirement of harmony and affection." Celnart speaks of moderation (remember *mediocrità*), sincerity, modesty, grace; she cites virtue ("love of good") as the soul of politeness. The spirit of her prescriptions is a far cry from the showy political manners of Louis XIV but no less detailed. Madame Celnart is *very* specific about what to do where and with whom: how to walk, talk, dress, visit, write letters, address servants, dine, sing, and on and on. One imagines tickets bearing rules like the ones at Versailles posted at every turn.

In a section called "Of The Toilet" (translated from *toilette* meaning style of dress) the author describes correct dress from bed clothes to ball gowns and the "rigorous simplicity of the dress of men." She specifies which fabrics to use, the cut of the garment, the accessories: "The dress for a man on his first rising, is a cap of cotton, or silk and cotton, a morning gown, or a vest with sleeves; for a lady, a small muslin cap, (*bonnet de percale*), a camisole or common gown." She cautions a young lady of "small fortune" to avoid embellishing simple clothes to make them more important than they are and "old ladies" to abstain from bright colors, high fashion, or ornaments like feathers and jewels. A "lady in her decline" must not look festive, decorated, or, for goodness sake, wear a dress with short sleeves. Old men should choose "grave colors" (*grave* colors, really?) for clothing a little out of style; and no wig. "Old persons should show their white and noble heads." Young people who go completely bald may wear wigs because nothing is sadder than "those bald skulls" that anatomists love to examine. "Propriety requires that we should always be clothed in a cleanly becoming manner, even in private, in leaving our bed, or in the presence of no one. It requires that our clothing be in keeping with our sex, fortune, profession, age, and form…The toilet wants harmony, which is the soul of elegance as well as beauty."

The table wants harmony, too. (At least mine does.) Celnart acknowledges that dining is almost "an event" due to the many rules of propriety the host and guests must follow, and inviting a congenial group of guests, or at least one that is tolerant of one another, is a good beginning. But don't forget the rules and essential details of deportment in the dining room, *very* important rules for how to enter and leave the room, seating, polite conversation, passing platters, and so forth. Of course, there are warnings: "It is ridiculous to make a display of your napkin; to attach it with pins upon your bosom, or to pass it through your buttonhole; to use a fork to eat soup…to cut bread with a knife which should be broken by your hand; and to pour coffee into the saucer to cool." Celnart writes that at the end of the meal ladies may dip their fingers into a glass of water and wipe them with the napkin, rinse the mouth and spit into the plate (*choquant! quelle horreur!*). Singing at the table: "We do not sing in the houses of people of fashion and the high classes of society; but we may do it at special tables of citizens." On that note...

The American Gentleman by Charles Butler, Esquire, of Philadelphia, published in 1836, is a collection of philosophical essays dedicated to points of etiquette that, like all books in this genre, records history. With broad strokes Butler paints a picture of early nineteenth-century America in the midst of social and economic change, the setting for a portrait of the ideal man in his time. Yet, it is impossible to look at Butler's picture of a uniquely American visage and ignore pentimenti, traces of previous works. Neoclassicism saturated American intellectual thought in the eighteenth and nineteenth centuries as it did in sixteenth-century Italy, and I see the "ghostings" (to use a word from the digital age) of Castiglione's courtier, of Della Casa's homespun uncle. I catch glimpses of Moody's puritanical moralist, too. Throughout the book there are quotes in Latin, references to and quotes by Cicero, Homer, Horace, Euclid, Ptolemy, to name a few.

As the author delineates his gentlemanly ideal he does not look to France or ancient Greece and Rome for his model but to his countryman. "Perhaps there is no word in our language to which so many meanings are attached as the word GENTLEMAN," he begins the introduction. Gentleman is a word used to describe a rich man who does not work for a living; a class of men who are second- and third-generation gentlemen, never mind how they gained the title; and there are the playboy types prone to elegant vices. Meanings fluctuate like fashion (a dirty word in his lexicon) and are "as changeable as the politics of a young patriot." But amidst the confusion of terms there is indeed a collection of traits that define genuine character as "distinctive and definite."

> To develop fully the beau ideal of an American
> gentleman, one should write whole volumes of sound
> morality, and whole treatises on that genuine polite-

ness which has its foundation in kindness of heart and purpose. To present a model for our countrymen, we have only to refer to our own Washington, who united dignity and polish with genuine excellence of soul which mark the true gentleman. He needed no patent from the hand of royalty. He was knighted by a nobler hand than Bayard's. He was stamped by the touch of his Maker with that impress which marked him "the choice and master spirit of his age."

Sadly, Washington's age had passed and for Butler, commerce and consumerism were corrupting American morals and manners and threatened core republican values. Butler advocates for temperance, punctuality, thrift, and above all "sincerity of heart." He ridicules the newly rich merchant, shaming him for abandoning a "noble mansion on a venerable old street" for a "smart" house in a new suburb; he rails against the "tyrant fashion" in all its iterations, from manners to clothes, books, buildings, and gardens, and denounces those who are enslaved to "her;" he seeks every opportunity to ridicule ceremonious behavior, dissimulation, and pretentiousness. The worst-bred person in company is the "superficial young man" who travels abroad and returns with "a bigotry of forms" and new fashions to put on airs. Good manners is "the art of remembering, and applying, certain settled forms of general behavior." Just a modicum of reason without acculturation naturally instructs good behavior. Good breeding is more complicated: "for besides an uncommon degree of literature sufficient to qualify a gentleman for reading a play, or a political pamphlet, it taketh a great compass of knowledge; no less than that of dancing, fighting, gaming, making the circle of Italy, riding the great horse, and speaking French..." [remember Castiglione's Renaissance gentleman].

Bushman reports that before 1800 American publishers issued eighteen versions of Lord Chesterfield's *Letters*. Readers who would never experience life as Chesterfield did "glean what they could for themselves as they attempted to make small courts of their drawing rooms and parlors." For Butler, Chesterfield's art of pleasing is a plague. "The professed students of the art of pleasing as taught in the Chesterfieldian system…are peculiarly unpleasing and extremely offensive." He says that the urge to study this "celebrated art" is unmitigated greed. To the rhetorical question of the price Chesterfield's followers pay to reach their goal, Butler replies from his pulpit that "the perpetual agitation of spirits, the tormenting fears, and the ardent hopes, which alternately disorder the bosom of the subtle and suspicious worldling" will more than outweigh the riches. What good are money, mansions, carriages if the one who chases after them has "worn out his sensibility, ruined his nerves, lost his eyes, and perhaps stained his honour and wounded his conscience, in toilsome drudgery and abject servitude, from his youth up even to the age of feebleness and decrepitude?" Butler all but says that the duplicitous Chesterfieldian's teeth will fall out and his house will burn down. Ecclesiastes 1:14 comes to mind: "…all is vanity and vexation of the spirit." If that fire and brimstone sermon were not enough, he offers a wacky essay to further attack Chesterfield: "A Dialogue of the Dead between Cicero and Lord Chesterfield." In tiny letters below the title is a Latin phrase that always gives me goose bumps: *esse quam videri*. Featured prominently on the seal of North Carolina and in the hearts of its citizens, it means "to be rather than to seem to be." Cicero speaks first: "Mistake me not. I know how to value the sweet courtesies of life. Affability, attention, decorum of behaviour, if they have not been ranked virtues, are certainly related to them, and have a powerful influence in promoting social happiness…but…to be truly amiable, they must proceed from goodness of heart.—Assumed by the artful to serve the purpose of private interest, they degenerate to contemptible grimace, and detestable hypocrisy." Chesterfield replies that he doesn't have time to respond because he has many social engagements including a rendezvous with his "little elegant French Comtesse." Cicero snaps: "Contemptible fop!" And the debate begins. You may be able to guess that Cicero—the moral gentleman "with open, sincere, and manly character"—is victorious.

Speaking of politeness elsewhere in the book, Butler explains his own art of pleasing as the responsibility of humankind to try to make oneself "agreeable to those in whose company we are destined to travel in the journey of life...it is one of our most important duties as men, and particularly required in the professor of Christianity."

Returning to one of his central themes—the effects of commerce on American morals—he writes the essay "On Supporting the Dignity of the Commercial Character." Since our situation has rendered America "naturally commercial, it is good policy to place the mercantile profession in an honourable light." In most countries the profession has been disgraced by "covetousness and circumvention," and its main goal, the accumulation of money, has never been highly regarded by "those who have seen the beauty of disinterested patriotism and heroic generosity." He chastises the men of his day for relinquishing the simplicity of the American character to "import the airs and manners of court into a counting-house." In doing so they lost their independence and dignity. He declares it time to return to the principle and manners that have been forgotten "in the pursuit of innovation [industrialization]."

The Victorians and Modern Manners

During the industrial revolution and the reign of Victoria and Albert, a newfound prudery and "a new sense of righteousness" were evident, says Pine-Coffin. "Victorianism" was fundamentally a middle-class outlook and not simply a consequence of the industrial revolution and increased wealth. The ethnocentric British were proud of their wealth but more importantly of their perceived racial and moral pre-eminence. Pine-Coffin continues, "It was this belief that determined their manners, for whatever may have been the true state of their morals—and they were certainly much better than their grandfathers—the Victorians were determined that their outward behavior at least should do full justice to the fine conception they had of themselves and their mission. If they were to succeed, they had to insist on the very strictest standards of formal etiquette, and a society such as theirs provided a very good market for instructional books containing the rules of good form, like the ritual of a new religion."

A proliferation of Victorian etiquette books explained every iota of comportment: dress, speech, hygiene, table manners, dancing, letter writing. *All About Etiquette; or The Manners of Polite Society* by Samuel Orchart Beeton, published in 1875, begins with the disclaimer that an introduction is not necessary because the title says it all. However, the author adds that "points in the polite code" previously overlooked are included. "We have endeavored to enter further than has yet been done into the detail of every branch of etiquette, as it is in small matters, in what are thought the trifling courtesies of everyday life, that good or bad breeding becomes conspicuous." It's no surprise that the table of contents has sixty different topic entries, many about the table. His wife, Isabella Beeton, was the Martha Stewart of her day, famous for her articles published from 1859 to 1861 as monthly supplements in S. O. Beeton's *Englishwoman's Domestic Magazine*. Those articles were combined into one volume and published as *Mrs. Beeton's Book of Household Management* in 1862. More than a thousand pages explain mainly "cookery"—recipes, menus, table settings—and there are a few, incidental chapters on child rearing, housekeeping, managing household finances, and training servants. On my bookshelf dedicated to cookbooks and dictionaries, I have Martha Stewart's *Housekeeping Handbook* and, to my great surprise, a food-stained copy of *Mrs. Beeton's Book of Household Management* that belonged to my mother.

Manners And Tone of Good Society; or Solecisms To Be

Avoided, published in 1879, was written by "A Member of the Aristocracy." No kidding. This is how the anonymous writer identified himself. In a short preface he laments the lack of space to expound upon "conversing with ease," polite conversation, or the so-called "small talk" of society. "Tact and innate refinement," he says, is a gift to very few (like Castiglione's grace, "those who have it from the stars"): lovely and helpful to people unacquainted with "society" but insufficient without knowledge of customs. The intent of the book is "rules and reference," to explain in excruciating detail *how* to be and *what* to do. Of course, I turned directly to chapter 6, "Dinner Parties—Dinner Giving and Dining Out." He begins, "DINNER-PARTIES rank first among all entertainments.... An invitation to dinner conveys a greater mark of esteem, or friendship and cordiality, towards the guest invited, than is conveyed by an invitation to any other social gathering, it being the highest compliment, socially speaking, that is offered by one person to another. It is also a civility that can be readily interchanged, which in itself gives it an advantage over *all* other civilities." A dinner party is a gift to the guests. It involves hard work that you need to love. Party or intimate dinner, an invitation to share a meal is a compliment.

Mr. Member of the Aristocracy (why do I think he is a man?) provides every detail of table decoration, setting the cutlery, glasses, seating of guests, how to walk in and out of the dining room and with whom. The "cover," as he calls it, describes the table setting of cutlery the same for small and large dinners: "Two large knives, and a silver knife and fork for fish, a table-spoon for soup, three large forks, a glass for sherry, a glass for hock, and a glass for champagne." The napkin is placed between the knives and forks in the middle of the setting and the bread is wrapped in the napkin. Because there was always a butler and footmen to serve courses, the dessert fork and spoon are presented on the empty dessert plate. It is the rule today that no more than three knives and three forks should be on the right and left of the table setting at one time. A fourth fork, the small cocktail fork, is the exception to this rule. Tablespoons are for the soup course and are placed on the right with the knives. Much of Mr. Aristocrat's detail is familiar and still the accepted formal way of doing things that Emily Post wrote about in *Etiquette* in 1955, the manners bible for generations of Americans, and that Amy Vanderbilt covered in *Complete Book of Etiquette* in 1952. What one learns from this is that the mechanics of dining and presentation, at least in the western world, have changed remarkably little over the past 150 years.

One tradition Mr. Aristocrat describes reminds me of a memorable personal experience. I was a twenty-four-year-old bride on my wedding trip to London when my husband and I were invited to the country for the weekend. A dinner party was given in our honor. At the end of dinner while all were still chatting at the table, the host unobtrusively signaled his wife who made a coquettish remark in "code." The women rose all at once to leave the table. Never mind that my exposure to polite behavior was pretty sophisticated, I did not get the cue. I stayed seated, that is, until the iron-butterfly hostess, an older belle from Atlanta, Georgia, walked with feline stealth to the back of my chair and with a firm, two-handed grip on my shoulders removed me to the drawing room. "Let's leave the men to themselves, Dahlin'," she purred in that southern drawl that masks determination. The men stayed at table for coffee, a round of wine, and to smoke cigars or cigarettes before joining the ladies in the drawing room. (If Chaucer thought the Prioress's French manners were affected, what would he say about this in the 1970s?) I have never forgotten this moment nor have I ever again participated in this archaic postprandial ritual, or wanted to.

The Ladies' Book of Etiquette, and Manual of Politeness by Florence Hartley (1860) is an American courtesy book that tempered my memory of the southern belle hostess in England. What I know now is that for an American lady of a certain age and social class, leaving the table to the men after dinner wasn't an affectation but rather a dinner ritual passed down from one generation to the next—even in America. "Coffee follows the dessert," Hartley writes, "and when this enters, if your guests are gentlemen only, your duty is at an end. You may then rise, leave the room, and need not re-appear. If you have lady guests, give the signal for rising after coffee, and lead the way to the parlor, where, in a few moments, the gentlemen will again join you." Of course Hartley also cautions her polite ladies, "Gloves and mittens are no longer worn at the table, even at the largest dinner-parties." Mittens at the table? Customs do change! Yet much of Hartley's advice is timeless, consistent with eighteenth-century as well as nineteenth- and twentieth-century American and Continental manners. Consider a few of her do's and don'ts: "Never attempt to touch any dish that is upon the table, but out of reach, by stretching out your arms, leaning forward, or, still worse, standing up. Ask the waiter to hand it, if you wish for it; or, if the gentleman beside you can easily do so, you may ask him to pass it to you." Still a no-no is holding forks and knives perpendicular to the plate and gesturing with cutlery: "When conversing let your knife and fork rest easily upon your plate, even if still in your hand. Avoid holding them upright." She cautions that eating should be noiseless (sound familiar?): "To munch or smack the lips are vulgar faults." Calm down when you get to the table: "Avoid stiffness, but at the same time, be careful that you do not annoy others by your restlessness." This includes eating so fast "as to be done before others," but don't eat so slowly that the table has to wait and watch you finish. And I love this: "To carry away fruit or bonbons from the table is a sign of low breeding."

Everyman's Encyclopaedia of Etiquette: What to Do, What to Say, What to Write, What to Wear: A Book of Manners for Everyday Use, in two volumes, by Emily Holt (1901, 1915, 1920 editions), has a distinctly American tone and differs from its British predecessors. The democratic title that speaks to "everyman" reflects American opposition to stylized manners, and optimism that through education and practice, every one of us can learn manners. Though Mrs. Holt's title is inclusive, she insists on following "the rules"—old-school rules inevitably influenced by British and Continental styles. Balls and debutante parties, engraved invitations, and training of servants, all of which she dissects, are hardly useful topics for "everyman." Dancing delicately around class differences and certainly never implying that she is Mrs. Aristocrat, the author unabashedly speaks of breeding. "Whether it is a family dinner without guests or a formal occasion, a man shows courtesy and breeding by waiting for the ladies to assume their seats." She describes posture at the table: "nothing so marks the well-bred man or woman as repose at table." Mrs. Holt's instruction is consistent with the earliest courtesy books and with the fundamentals of table manners still honored today. "One should sit erect, and neither lounge nor bend forward while eating." She explains how to use the napkin: "none but the vulgarian tucks his napkin in the top of his waistcoat." She warns that it is a sign of "careless training" to mash food between the fork prongs or to mix a lot of different foods together and pile them onto the fork and "shovel" into the mouth. A "noiseless and deliberate eating" style is evidence of respect for one's health and personal dignity. "Only the underbred or uneducated bolt their food, strike their spoon, fork, or glass against their teeth, suck up a liquid from a spoon, clash knives and forks against their plates, scrape the bottom of a cup, plate, or glass in hungry pursuit of a last morsel, and masticate with the mouth open, pat the top of a pepper pot to force out the contents and drum on a knife-blade in order to distribute salt or meat or vegetables." Were it not for the inclusion of forks, plates, and glass, this could as easily be "do's and don'ts" for the medieval knight and squire as for the twentieth-century person!

The American bare-bones mindset of today is a throwback to our Protestant forefathers, Puritans who distrusted religious and social ritual and believed that art was deceitful and sophistication was a kind of moral pollution. Indirection and tact? Brutal honesty was virtuous. Judith Martin writes in *Miss Manners' Guide to Excruciatingly Correct Behavior*: "Until recent years, people strove for perfection, and the person who achieved it was universally admired and imitated.... Now, however, it is our faults for which we are loved. Imperfect table manners are considered a sign of subscribing to the principles of democracy; ignorance of high culture to be an indication of spirituality; and blurting rough speech to be a clue to perfect honesty."

Americans have always valued individualism over the group, but bring this attitude to the dinner table and you have pigsty style, every man for himself without regard for social interaction. We insist on the casual dinner (monotonous simplicity that would make a Puritan sing), which has few rules and suspends judgment of performance. Yes, this informality is economical in a world without servants, and it can be seen as fallout from the 1960s when "rules" went out the window along with bras, hats, and white gloves, and the intelligentsia, championing social reform, donned the worker's blue denim costume. Jeans became the sexless, classless garment that offered freedom of movement and economic accessibility, and once gentrified evolved into a fashion statement—the designer version priced in the hundreds of dollars—and a must for every wardrobe. We can thank Levi Strauss for this sartorial creation inspired by the gold rush of 1849. First made of brown wagon tenting, the protective overalls were soon made of the even tougher cotton fabric dyed indigo and called *serge de Nîmes* from the south of France. *"De Nîmes"* mispronounced by American dock workers became "denim;" "jeans" comes from Genes, French for the Italian port of Genoa from which denim was shipped to Strauss in San Francisco. The naysayers of today, many of whom came of age in that tumultuous decade and sport their blue jeans to this day, bristle at the mention of etiquette and view table manners as folderol—the persnickety purview of the humorless, didactic spinster aunt who holds her tea-cup with the pinkie finger erect and would rather offer you a firm enema than sugar in your tea.

Mrs. Holt's etiquette and no-nonsense tone contribute to this prim, Victorian stereotype. Holt embraces modernity in a chapter called "Sport," with the subheading "Automobile and Carriage Courtesy," to instruct the man driving a woman in his automobile or carriage how to behave. "Etiquette for Women Drivers" describes in elaborate detail how to get into the car or carriage, what clothes to wear, and what courteous gestures to make. "While driving [in a horse-drawn carriage], she bows as does a man, by touching her hat's brim with the stock of her whip; while motoring with the conventional inclination of her head." In twenty-first-century America we have *jetiquette* that establishes the rules of polite behavior while traveling in a private jet; *netiquette* to define what constitutes polite communication via e-mail; and *tech-etiquette* guiding the courteous use of iPods, cell phones, and cameras, however they are configured. Social media etiquette preaching respect for privacy issues and discouraging over-sharing is brand new and championed by none other than Facebook creator Mark Zuckerberg's sister Randi. At my gym placards posted on the tile walls of the pool read "The Etiquette of Lap Swimming" and spell out swimming patterns and urge courteous consideration of those sharing your lane. In New York City subway cars are decorated with large posters with bold print, "Courtesy Counts. Be someone who makes it a better ride for everyone. Manners make a better ride." A series of tickets or cards with drawings and tag lines placed high on the walls above the posters explain do's and don'ts of subway etiquette. Executive manners receive the most attention and have inspired a whole industry pumping out books to bring business men and women up to speed. These "etiquettes" prove that our need for structure and considerate behavior always finds expression—that is, dress—one way or another.

On the heels of Mrs. Holt came Margaret Bailey's *The Value of Good Manners*, published in 1922. The author reiterates all the reasons why Americans are suspicious of refinement and considers the uphill battle, asking, "Are Good Manners worth the price?" Optimistic about the American experiment, she replies: "Fortunate it is, then, that manners are but one of the common privileges of a democracy; that just because there is no class distinction, they are within the reach of all. For, by their exercise, as in no other way, a man may win his business and his social rank."

~

The late William C. Friday was an American educator raised in the small town of Dallas, North Carolina. He served as president of the University of North Carolina for thirty years, achieved political power unprecedented in the state, and received national recognition for his progressive ideas. Among the most revered men of his generation and a model of gentlemanly behavior, Mr. Friday dressed in coat and tie, stood up when a woman entered the room, spoke of friends with deference using the titles Mr. or Mrs. He expressed courtesy naturally, gracefully: the Renaissance terms *sprezzatura* and *leggiadria* come to mind. "Courage, manners, and decency cost a person so little," he said in a 1995 Associated Press interview. "But disregard them and see what you get."

In October 2012, as my sister and I walked with our family to the campus for William Friday's memorial service, we passed the Old Well, a small classical structure that covers a water fountain where once a ground well stood. Now a symbol of the university, the well that day was dressed in flowers, billowing bouquets brought by mourners—students, faculty, and Chapel Hill residents alike. Leaning against the floral covering was a large homemade sign that read, "Farewell to the last Southern gentleman." I imagined that a student in the adjacent dormitory spontaneously scribbled his or her good-bye. Although Bill Friday retired as president many years before the current undergraduate population was even born, students of every generation knew him. He, in turn, not only remembered their names but took a genuine interest in them as he did with all of us. In fact, his eulogy read by the present university president Tom Ross sounded like passages from *The Courtier*, so multifaceted were his talents and seemingly effortless his accomplishments. Bill Friday and his family were lifelong neighbors and close friends to me and my family. We shared dinners, travels, everyday life. I witnessed the depth and constancy of his generosity and his thoughtfulness in small things at times when few, if any, were watching.

We have not seen the last of the southern gentlemen, of this I am certain. At the university my young men and women friends from all walks of life in the north, south, and in between are eager to learn manners as they prepare for careers. These are the ladies and gentlemen of the future. Some, whose parents have taken the time to teach comportment, already practice the old-fashioned and thoughtful customs of holding doors, gentlemen walking on the street side when in the company of women, and handwriting thank-you notes. These are highly intelligent, well-educated, technologically skilled young adults who have but one missing link—basic knowledge of the table. I am optimistic that whatever is lacking in the table manners department can be restored, and that this book will be the ticket.

References

"The ABC of Aristotle." [ca. 1430] 1908. In *The Babees' Book*, by Edith Rickert. London: Chatto and Windus.

Axtell, Roger. 1991. *Gestures: The Do's and Taboos of Body Language around the World*. New York: John Wiley and Sons.

"The Babees' Book or A Little Report of How Young People Should Behave." [ca. 1475] 1908. In *The Babees' Book*, by Edith Rickert. London: Chatto and Windus.

Bailey, Margaret Emerson. 1922. *The Value of Good Manners: Practical Politeness in the Daily Concerns of Life*. New York: Doubleday, Page & Company.

Baldridge, Letitia. 1990. *Complete Guide to the New Manners for the 90's*. New York: Rawson and Associates.

———. 1993. *New Complete Guide to Executive Manners*. New York: Macmillan Publishing Company.

Beeton, Samuel Orchart. 1875. *All About Etiquette; or, The Manners of Polite Society*. London: Ward, Lock and Company.

Berger, Harry, Jr. 2002. "Sprezzatura and the Absence of Grace." In *The Book of the Courtier: Singleton Translation*, edited by Daniel Javitch. New York and London: W. W. Norton and Company.

"The Book of Courtesy." [ca. 1350] 1908. In *The Babees' Book*, by Edith Rickert. London: Chatto and Windus.

Brousseau, Jim, ed. 2002. *Social Graces: Words of Wisdom on Civility in a Changing Society*. New York: Hearst Communications.

Brown, Patricia Fortini. 2004. *Private Lives in Renaissance Venice*. New Haven: Yale University Press.

Bushman, Richard L. 1993. *The Refinement of America*. New York: Vintage Books.

Butler, Charles. 1836. *The American Gentleman*. Philadelphia: Hogan and Thompson.

Castiglione, Baldesar. [1528] 2002. *Il Cortegiano (The Book of the Courtier)*. Translated by Charles S. Singleton. New York: Norton Critical Editions.

Celnart, Elisabeth. 1833. *The Gentleman and Lady's Book of Politeness and Propriety of Deportment: dedicated to the youth of both sexes; translated from the sixth Paris edition, enlarged and improved*. Boston: Allen and Ticknor and Carter, Hendee.

Chaucer, Geoffrey. [ca. 1395] 2003. *The Canterbury Tales*. Translated by Nevill Coghill. London: Penguin Classics.

Chesterfield, Earl of. [1774] 2008. *Lord Chesterfield's Letters to His Son*. Edited with an introduction and notes by David Roberts. New York: Oxford University Press.

Coryat, Thomas. 1611. *Coryat's Crudities*. Printed by William Stansby for the author.

Deetz, James. 1996. *In Small Things Forgotten: An Archaeology of Early American Life*. New York: Anchor Books.

Della Casa, Giovanni. [1558] 1986. *Il Galateo, or About Manners*. Translated by Konrad Eisenbichler and Kenneth R. Bartlett. Toronto: Centre for Reformation and Renaissance Studies.

D'Epiro, Peter, and Mary Desmond Pinkowish. 2001. *Sprezzatura: 50 Ways Italian Genius Shaped the World*. New York: Anchor Books.

George Washington's Rules of Civility and Decent Behavior. 2007. Naperville, Illinois: Sourcebooks.

Hartley, Florence. 1860. *The Ladies' Book of Etiquette and Manual of Politeness*. Boston: G.W. Cottrell, Publisher.

Hawkins, Francis. [1668] 2010. *Youth's Behaviour, or Decency in conversation amongst men composed in French by grave persons, for the use and benefit of their youth; now newly turned into English by Francis Hawkins*. EEBO Editions, ProQuest.

Holt, Emily. 1920. *Everyman's Encyclopaedia of Etiquette: What to Do, What to Say, What to Write, What to Wear: A Book of Manners for Everyday Use*. New York: Holt, Page and Company.

Hoving, Walter. 1987. *Tiffany's Table Manners for Teenagers*. New York: Random House.

"How the Good Wife Taught her Daughter." [ca. 1350] 1908. In *The Babees' Book*, by Edith Rickert. London: Chatto and Windus.

Johnson, Dorothea. 1997. *The Little Book of Etiquette*. Philadelphia: The Running Press.

Kelly-Gadol, Joan. 2002. "Did Women Have a Renaissance?" In *The Book of the Courtier: Singleton Translation*, edited by Daniel Javitch. New York and London: W. W. Norton and Company.

La Bienséance de la conversation entre les hommes. [1595] 2010. Whitefish, Montana: Kessinger Publishing.

Mansel, Philip. 2005. *Dressed to Rule*. New Haven and London: Yale University Press.

Martin, Judith. 1982. *Miss Manners' Guide to Excruciatingly Correct Behavior*. New York: Galahad Books.

A Member of the Aristocracy. 1879. *Manners And Tone of Good Society; or Solecisms To Be Avoided*. London: Frederick Warne and Company.

Morgan, John. 1996. *Debrett's New Guide to Etiquette and Modern Manners*. New York: Thomas Dunne Books, St. Martin's Press.

Paston-Williams, Sara. 1993. *The Art of Dining: A History of Cooking and Eating*. London: National Trust Enterprises.

Pine-Coffin, R. S. 1958. "A Note on Books of Courtesy in England." In *Il Galateo*, by Giovanni Della Casa. Translated by R. S. Pine-Coffin. Harmondsworth, Middlesex, England: Penguin Books.

Post, Emily. 1955. *Etiquette*. 9th ed. New York: Funk and Wagnalls.

Rickert, Edith. 1908. *The Babees' Book: Medieval Manners for the Young: Done into Modern English from Dr. Furnival's Texts*. London: Chatto and Windus.

Russell, John. [ca. 1479] 1908. "John Russell's Book of Nurture." In *The Babees' Book*, by Edith Rickert. London: Chatto and Windus.

Seager, Francis. [ca. 1550] 1908. "Seager's School of Virtue." In *The Babees' Book*, by Edith Rickert. London: Chatto and Windus.

Shorter Oxford English Dictionary, 6th ed. 2007. New York: Oxford University Press.

Tuckerman, Nancy, and Nancy Dunnan. 1995. *The Amy Vanderbilt Complete Book of Etiquette Entirely Rewritten and Updated*. New York: Doubleday.

"Urbanitatis." [ca. 1450] 1908. In *The Babees' Book*, by Edith Rickert. London: Chatto and Windus.

Vanderbilt, Amy. 1952. *The Complete Book of Etiquette*. New York: Doubleday and Company.

Visser, Margaret. 1992. *The Ritual of Dinner: The Origins, Evolution, Eccentricities, and Meanings of Table Manners*. London: Penguin Books.

Weste, Richard. [1619] 1908. "Richard Weste's School of Virtue, The Second Part, or The Young Scholar's Paradise." In *The Babees' Book*, by Edith Rickert. London: Chatto and Windus.

Wilson, Charles Reagan. 1989. "Manners." In *Encyclopedia of Southern Culture*, edited by Charles Reagan Wilson and William Ferris. Chapel Hill: University of North Carolina Press.

Design and composition by Julie Allred, BW&A Books

Set in Cochin, a serif Italian old-style typeface
designed in 1912 by Georges Peignot and named
for an eighteenth-century French engraver,
Charles-Nicolas Cochin le Jeune (the Younger).

Manufactured in Lillington, North Carolina,
by Edwards Brothers Malloy